Stamper Footprints

Eleven Generations

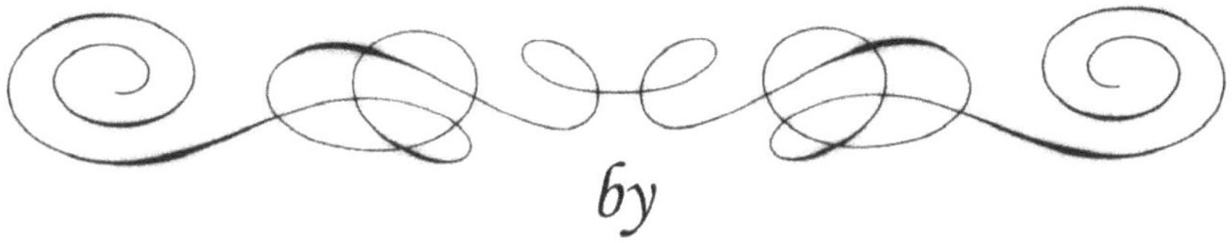

by

Betty Stamper Latham

HERITAGE BOOKS
2013

HERITAGE BOOKS
AN IMPRINT OF HERITAGE BOOKS, INC.

Books, CDs, and more—Worldwide

For our listing of thousands of titles see our website
at
www.HeritageBooks.com

Published 2013 by
HERITAGE BOOKS, INC.
Publishing Division
100 Railroad Ave. #104
Westminster, Maryland 21157

International Standard Book Numbers
Paperbound: 978-0-7884-0320-0
Clothbound: 978-0-7884-6907-7

ACKNOWLEDGEMENTS

It has been an exciting experience finding out as much as possible about my father's ancestors, the STAMPERS. I want to share this information with you so I have put together this little book. I could not have accomplished this without the help of many people. First, I want to thank my daughter Georgia Sue Latham, M.D. who got me started in family research, and so graciously helped with the editing. I thank my husband, George, for all his help and for going with me on many adventurous trips in search of my past. Without his help, I could not have gotten this accomplished. He helped with the research and the editing. For those who had done much research before me and graciously shared their information with me, I would like to tell them here how much I appreciate everything they did. Doctor Clifford Stamper, my cousin, who not only shared his information but also told me how to go about doing research on my own, "I thank you so very much". Thank you, to Samuel E. Sebastian and his wife Hallie who not only shared the research of thirty years but who have become good friends. Thank you, to James J. Stamper for sharing his information with me. Thank you, Colonel Lynn B. Moore, of Fairfax, Virginia, who did much research for our family. I thank my aunts, Irene Stamper Moore Gilbuena and Macle Stamper Shore and my cousins Nancy Miles Royal, Louise Miles Evans, John Edward Stamper and his wife Cora Mae, Tom Miles and his wife Shirley, Norma Stamper Starr and Elaine Stamper Greenburg for their help. I have received so much help and information from family and friends, for those who are not acknowledged here, I want to say "Thank you" for sharing the information of your families with me.

GEORGE HENRY AND BETTY STAMPER LATHAM

DEDICATED TO

My sister **SHIRLEY STAMPER HARRIS** who gives meaning to the word Family.

and

To those members of my family who have gone before, are here now and are yet to come.

INTRODUCTION

To go back in time and know our ancestors would be the greatest of all adventures. Since time travel is not yet possible, we are forced to find out about our ancestors by researching and researching. Spending hours in dimly lit rooms, peering into the screen and turning the crank of the microfilm reader. We search the archives of the past in pursuit of truths concerning the ones who went before us, visiting courthouses and libraries searching through old records and old books, writing many letters to relatives and other people with the same name, learning all we can from former researchers and genealogists. We do this because it is of importance for us to know about our ancestors and leave a record for the generations to come.

The early pioneers lived their lives from day to day, and trusted in the Almighty God to provide for the future. The business of just keeping alive was often a matter of great achievement in itself. They often could not read and write and the records they left were no more then were required by their churches and the law. Many of the meager records that were left have been lost in county courthouse fires, floods, and in many cases were thrown out by people who did not want to keep any thing old whether it had meaning for others or not. For these reasons, it is hard to know the whole truth from part truths.

Every effort has been made to make this as a complete and accurate record as possible. However errors are inevitable, even with the greatest of care. If you find mistakes I would be grateful if you would let me know about them, so I can correct them in my records.

Each person appears in two locations in the text. The first as a child, the second as the head of a family group. When the person appears as the head of a family group, the name will be in capital letters followed by the anastral line with numbers after each name. An example, following a person's anastral line for five generations:

ONLEY EUGENE^{5} STAMPER, (John Ander^{4}), (Troy^{3}), (John^{2}), (Jonathan Jr.^{1}).

This numbering system will let the reader know from which generation the person is from.

The name Stamper appears in Denmark 500-1000 AD. Then moved to Normandy around 1000, then to England with the Norman invasion in 1066. The name probably came from one who was a stamper of coins.

CHAPTER 1

ANCESTRY

The ancestry of the **STAMPER** family is based on much research by several persons over many years. The first records that we have in Middlesex County, Virginia are of John Stamper, who appears to be the immigrant ancestor from England. We are not sure of his birth date or the date he arrived in the Colony of Virginia, but he appeared in the area that became Middlesex County around 1660.

It is presumed that **JOHN STAMPER** was the immigrant ancestor and that he was from England. This is based on two facts; First the majority of early settlers in Middlesex County were of English origin. Second copies of John Stamper's hand writing points to English rather then Colonial origins or any other country[16].

Since there are no birth or baptismal records for John or his sons John and Powell, we could rationalize that they were not born in Middlesex County, Virginia. No records have been found from ship list when they entered the colony. What would make one believe they came from England? At the time they lived in Middlesex County, Virginia, it was an English colony. The English government encouraged families to go to the colonies.

Ships came regularly to Middlesex County up the Rappahannock River from England to bring goods to trade and to take the tobacco back to England. Since no other records can be found we have to draw some conclusions. There are three or four Johns named in record books from Christ Church Parish, and it is not possible to know without any doubt, which is father, son or brother. Dates in the Church records are of some help in distinguishing one John from the other but not much.

We can not be sure of the name of John Stamper's wife. From the records of Christ Church, we find, "Dorcas Stamper wife of John departed this world July 16, 1667" [1]. It is believed that this was the wife of the first John Stamper of Middlesex county, Virginia, and the mother of our line of the Stampers. Dorcas's death record is the earliest date listed for any Stamper in the Register.

One could surmise that our first John married someone named Elizabeth, (last name could not be read when Register was copied) after Dorcas died. As we find in the Register, "Elizabeth -------wife of, John Stamper, died 29 April 1683 [1]." It could be possible that the son of our first John, is the John named here.

There is still a possible third marriage for our John or it could have been his second marriage. Listed in the Register of Christ Church of Middlesex County, Virginia is; "John married Carew (Cary) 8 May 1684 [1]". Carew is named in John Stamper's will as loving wife Carew Stamper.

He was listed as being in the Militia 23 November 1687 (ref. Colonial Militia). Extracts from the county records of Middlesex County, Virginia, military census 1687, page 189: "John Stamper, thought by this court capable to serve as footman and to fend with arms."

John was both a planter and carpenter. At least he had enough expertise in carpentry that he was requested by the vestry and the court to view the quality of carpentry work done by others[16].

We find the Stamper names in the Vestry Book of Christ Church Parish. From the Vestry Book of Christ Church Parish, page 56, on October 10, 1687, "It is ordered by this p'sent Vestry y' Mr Oswald Cary P'sent Ch. warden to be paid for Carpenters Work done at y' Gre`t Church by Mr. John Stamper. 100 lb Tob [4]." From this we see that John did carpentry work as well as grow tobacco. He was paid for the carpenter work done on the church in tobacco instead of money. So we can see that the county used tobacco as a substitute for money.

John Stamper was a literate man. At one time he was a Major in the Lancaster Militia, early records refer to him as "Mr.". He entertained Minister John Shepherd in his home in 1679, and he knew Richard Robinson well enough to have named him guardian to his son John[16].

There has not been found a deed showing when and how this first John Stamper obtained his land, but is known that his parcel contained 200 acres. This land was in the northeastern side of the county[16]. The county map of Middlesex County still shows the community of Stamper, and Stamper's Landing, they are located in the southeastern part of the county, beside the Piankatank River.

Today Stamper's Landing has only a pier from which one could fish or tie up a boat. We visited there on a cool spring morning. It had just stopped raining and the mist was rising over the river. There is a bend in the river, it is wide where the bend is and a little island (Berkley Island) could be seen through the mist. The beauty of it took my breath away. In my mind's eye, through the mist, I could see John Stamper, in a boat coming up the river. He was looking for the land he would claim to plant tobacco and build a home. The trees grow down to the river and the land would have to be cleared to plant the tobacco. This was a beautiful place to build a home and there would be plenty of fish and game for food. He did not know what to expect. Were the Indians friendly? What kinds of wild animals were there? He could only imagine the hardships of pioneer life.

The above facts give us something to wonder about. Did John first own land at Stamper's Landing and later obtain land in the northeastern part of the county? Or it could have been, he first owned land in the northeastern part of the county and later in time obtained land at Stamper's Landing.

There is no way we can know for sure how the Stampers of

Middlesex County lived, but by looking at the history of the County we can imagine how they may have lived. The Colony of Virginia was very young. The first English settlement in Jamestown was in 1607, but those first settlers had returned to England in 1615. It was 1618, after a new Governor of the Virginia Company (colony) was assigned, that private property was instituted[3].

Tobacco was a minor rage in England and in order to attract settlers to the colony to grow tobacco, in 1618 "Headright" was instituted, the right of an individual to claim fifty acres of land for each "head" for whom he paid the cost of transportation to the colony[3]. We can speculate that these first Stampers paid their transportation over from England and were able to claim some land. Every family raised tobacco to ship to England. At that time, tobacco was also used in the county in place of money [3].

Middlesex County of the Colony of Virginia was so accessible by ship that it was settled in the 1640's. Most of the early colonists were from London, England and the surrounding shire known as Middlesex; thus the name Middlesex County, Virginia. The official origin of Middlesex County is 2 February 1673 because that is the date of the first extant court records[16].

The ships that took the tobacco to England brought back things that the people needed and could not get in the colonies, such as glass for the windows of the houses, nails, tools, shoes, ready made clothes, and fine cloth to make dresses, etc[3].

The average family lived in a small weatherboard house with one or two rooms, there was a loft for the children and any house servants to sleep. The larger of the two rooms had a fireplace at one end which was used for heat and cooking. It was in this room that the family lived and entertained. When there was a second smaller room it was the bedroom of the husband and wife. Otherwise the large room was also used for the bedroom.

Out beside the house there was a family garden. There was a chicken coop for a few chickens and a barn for the cow. Some families had a few sheep for wool and two or three pigs[3].

Tobacco was the way of life. Every family member, except for very small children, helped in the growing of the tobacco. Almost everyone over the age of seven smoked or used tobacco in some way[3].

Most families had bond servants in the early settlements and later black slaves. The first tobacco farming was done the same as the Indians had done, with the labor of people without the aid of oxen or horses.

Most of the land was covered with large trees. The land had to cleared of the trees. The ground around the stumps was dug up with hoes, and the tobacco was planted in hills. The early settlers cultivated the tobacco as the Indians did. Tobacco demanded intensive labor at particular times of the year. After the seed beds were in, there was time to plant corn. Corn was the main food crop for people and cattle. By the time the corn was in the ground, it was time to pull the tobacco plants and transfer them to the hills of soil, where they would grow during the summer. The work of the tobacco was just begun, it was late fall before the tobacco was graded and packed ready to ship to England.

One would think that now there would be time for some rest. Oh no! Now more land needed to be cleared for the next years planting. The cycle started over, the work of growing tobacco was never done[3].

Game was plentiful and in our mind's eye we can see our ancestors going out to hunt food for their dinner, after a long day of working in the fields. The river had an abundance of fish, the older children would do the fishing.

To add to the hardship of colonial life, there were the Indians who were not too friendly. The Indians were the reason the Militia was needed.

The Christ Church Parish (Episcopal Church) was a very important part of the lives of the settlers of the county, it served as a place of worship and a place to socialize. The county had three chapels, upper, lower and middle. The middle chapel was called the Mother Church. Three chapels were needed as not ever family had horses and many would have to walk to the church. The Vestry-book of Christ Church, Middlesex, began in 1663 and ending 1767, it is now preserved at the Episcopal Theological Seminary, Alexander County, Virginia.

The Reverend John Shepherd was minister of the Parish from 1668 until the time of his death in 1683. We find in the Register of Christ Church Perish of Middlesex County, the names of our Stamper ancestors[1].

The Lower Chapel today belongs to the United Methodist. The first building was wood, the brick building standing today was to be finished 3 January 1716\17[15].

From Court Orders, Book No.1, 1673-1680 dated 2 February 1673, page 3: "Mary Grier, Daughter of Anner Grier is bound Apprenticed to John Stamper." This shows that John had one bound servant apprenticed, she more then likely was a helper around the house, helping with house work and the care of children. About a year after John's death, we find in the court orders on 6 April 1691: "Mary Grier, Apprenticed to John Stamper decd is this day discharged and set free and ordered to be paid Corne and Cloathes according to act"[16].

John Stamper's will was dated 9 November 1688, and at that time he named a son, John not yet of age. His son Powell is not named. Is this will the will of our first John, or could it possibly be the will of an older son of our first John, who was named John? With this John being the brother of Powell and their mother being Dorcas? More research needs to be done to prove or disprove some of these theories. All researchers of the Stampers agree that, the first John was married more then one time and had at least two sons Powell and John.

Here is a copy of a will, written by a John Stamper.

From: Wills Etc. 1676-1798, Pt, Compiled from papers Bundle 1, [by Betty M. Maynard].

In ye name of God Amen. I John Stamper of County of Middlesex being in good health of Body, and sound and pfect Mind and Memory, Praise be therefore given unto Almighty God, doe make and ordain this my present Last Will and Testament in manner for me following (that is to say) first and principally I Commend my Soul into ye hands of Almighty God, Hoping though ye Merits death and Passion of my Savior Jesus Christ to have full and free pardon and forgiveness of all my Sins, and to inherit everlasting Life, and my body I Commit to ye Earth to be decently buried at ye discretion of my Executors hereafter Named and as touching ye discretion of all Such Temporal Estate, As it hath pleased Almighty God to bestow upon me I give and dispose thereof as followeth: first I will that my debts and funeral charge shall be paid and discharged.

Item I do give and bequeath unto my Loving Wife Carew Stamper, and my Loving son John Stamper all my Temporal Estate that Lieth of Consisteth in goods and Chattels whatsoever Jointly between them both, whom I do leave my Joynt and Sole Executors of this my Last Will and Testament. Item I Leaveth Richard Robinson my Sons Guardian Item That my Loving Wife aforesaid Carew Stamper doe Injoy and possess the third part of all my Lands for her life, and in Case that my Son John die before he Commeth of Age my will is that my aforesaid wife Carew Stamper Shall Injoy and possess all my Lands to her and her heirs forever, and I doe hereby Revoke and disannul and make voide all former Wills and Testaments by me heretofore made. In Witness whereof I the said John Stamper to this my Last will and Testament Sett my hand and Seale, this ninth day of November one thousand Six hundred Eighty and Eight- 1688.

John Stamper (Seal)

Sealed and Delivered
in ye prests of
Robard Vallicott   George Wortham   William Vallicott

I see John Stamper as a man who came to the colony seeking a place to be free to worship God as he chose. In this new land he would claim wilderness land and make it into a plantation. He was a courageous man who served in the Militia, and fought in the minor Indian uprisings. He was married as few as once or maybe as many as three, and had at least two sons. He worked hard clearing land and planting tobacco. He attended services at the Christ Church Parish Chapel. Before going in the chapel for services he stood around outside the chapel and visited with the other men, smoking and talking about the problems they were having with the tobacco crop. Saturday outside the chapel and visited with the other men, smoking and talking about the problems they were having with the tobacco crop. Saturday night, he may have gone to the nearest ordinary (tavern), which was in someone's home, to drink a little ale and chat with his friends. They may have played cards or threw some darts. When the chapel needed repairs he was ready to do the work. John could read and write and was active in the affairs of the community. He had a quick temper which would flare up when something did not go right or when someone upset him. He was just as quick to forgive the shortcomings of others. He had more good then bad qualities, we can be proud to have had him for an ancestor.

No records have yet been found to establish the circumstances of John Stamper's death. The date we have for his death is March 1690 in Middlesex County, Virginia. He left his footprints in the fields where he grew his tobacco, and in the Church and Court Records of Middlesex County, Virginia.

STAMPER LANDING, MIDDLESEX COUNTY, VIRGINIA
(taken 7 March 1992)

CHRIST CHURCH PARISH, MIDDLESEX COUNTY, VIRGINIA
(taken March 7, 1992)

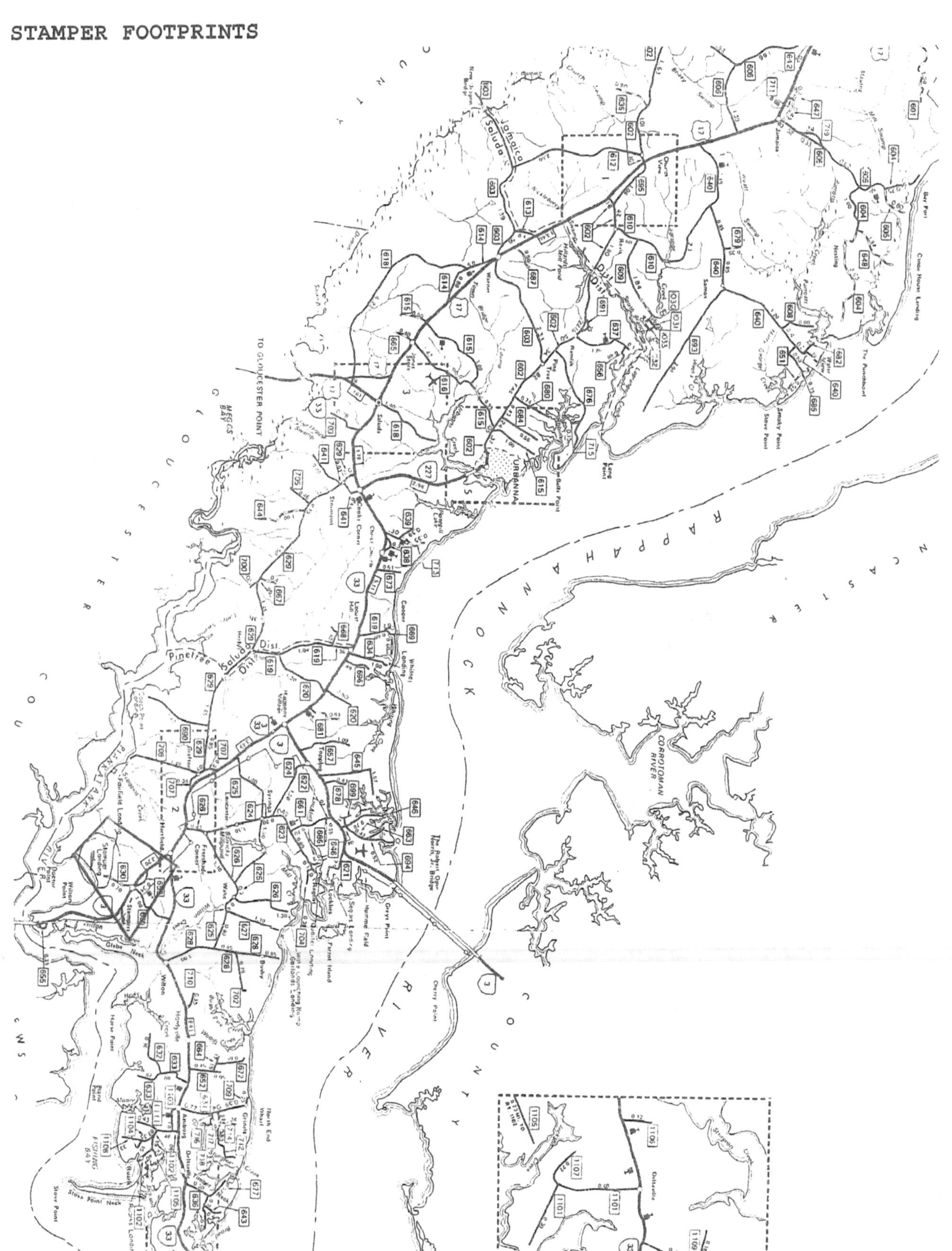

Map of Middlesex County, Virginia, courtesy of the Virginia Department of Transportation, showing Stampers and Stamper Landing.

CHAPTER 2

SECOND GENERATION

POWELL[2] STAMPER (John[1]) the ancestor of this line of STAMPER descendants, is believed to be the son of the immigrant from England John Stamper. We do not know his birth date. We find records of him in Middlesex County, Virginia in 1680, as well as a brother named John.

From a magazine "Stamper Stage" (September 1980 and December 1980) we find the conclusions of the ancestry of John's son Powell according to the research of many people. I personally find their conclusions confusing. To the best of my understanding, of their conclusions, Dorcas, wife of John, who died 16 July 1667 was Powell's mother. The John, whose wife, Elizabeth, died 29 April 1683 was Powell's older brother. Powell's brother John remarried, 8 May 1984, Carew---, from record's of Christ Church. Even though, it is hard to follow, I am inclined to go along with this theory until I have more facts. This would make the will of the John in the first chapter belong to the second John. The son named in the will, who was not yet of age would be the third John.

Powell married Mary Brooks on 10 April 1708, the record is at Christ Church Parish in Middlesex County, Virginia[1]. Mary's parents were Jonathan and Sarah Brooks, and she was born in 1687. From records of Christ Church Parish: "Mary daughter of Sarah widow of Jonathan Brooks bap'po, May 1687" [1]. This indicates that Mary's father died before she was born or soon after her birth. We have no record of Mary as a child and do not know if she had a step-father or not.

There is a copy of Jonathan Brooks' will from "Wills Etc. 1675-1798 P. 1, from loose papers bundle 1, [by Betty Maynard]."

In the name of God Amen. I Jonathan Brooks of the county of Middlesex being sick and weak in body do make this my last will and Testament. First I commit my soul to God which gave it and my body to the ground to be buried after such a decent manner as my companion shall think fit. Item: I give to my well beloved wife Saray Brook all my goods and chattels whatso over paying my debts and funeral expenses so long as she shall keep herself in my name. But if she shall marry again then all goods and chattels aforesaid to be equally divided among my children and she shall have an equal part thereof.

Witness my hand and seal this ____ January 1686
Jonathan Brooks Seal

Teste George Prestnall X William Mayo Probated 7 May 1687

We see from these dates of the will, that Mary was born the same month as the will was probated. She did have siblings as mentioned in the will.

From: (Stamper Court Records Middlesex County, Virginia 1673-1852) compiled by Betty M. Maynard; Powell Stamper inherited all of his fathers property, and with the exception of 100 acres he sold the rest of the land in 1711. The 100 acres which were left remained in the Stamper family until a James Stamper and Nancy Stamper Williams sold it to William F. Newcomb, October 1852[16]. This gives us yet another reason to believe the will of John Stamper's in chapter one was the Will of the Second John. There was no Powell named in that will.

I would like for us to use our imagination, to see if we can imagine what Powell and Mary's wedding was like. On her wedding day, Mary Brooks was twenty one, which was older then most girls of that time married. I imagine that Powell was several years older, as many as twenty. If Dorcas was his mother she died in 1667. As stated earlier we do not know his birth date. (According to information found in "A Place In Time Middlesex County, Virginia 1650-1750" by Darrett B. and Anita H. Rutman, only one percent of the males in the county lived past the age of fifty[3]. So if Powell was as old as forty at the time of his marriage his life expectancy was only about ten more years. Yet men of the time did marry at an older age as they wanted to be established with land and a house before marrying.

Now to the wedding, they could have had it at Mary's mother's house, with the Pastor riding his horse over to perform the service. Mary's mother, Sarah had made her wedding dress from fine cloth imported from England. It would be hard to tell how many pounds of tobacco it took to pay for the cloth. She had sewn it by hand and it had taken several weeks for her to finish it. The dress was trimmed with fine handmade lace. The early spring wild flowers were in bloom and Mary wore some in her hair. Her light brown hair was braided and then put up on top of her head and the flowers made a wreath around her head like a halo. Friends and near neighbors came to help celebrate the wedding. There was plenty of food and drink. The neighbor women had come to help Mary's mother fix the food, they also brought extra dishes and tankers (mugs). There was not room in the house for the wedding party, so tables were set up under the trees beside the house. They had killed a pig and some chickens, there was cornbread and a cake, and to drink there was apple cider and maybe even some beer and ale. After everyone had eaten, there was dancing to the music of a fiddle. The celebration went on most of the night. Powell had already built a two room weatherboard house with a fireplace, and there was a loft for the children they would have.

The house Powell had built, was furnished with a bed, some chests, a table, and a few chairs. There were a few pots and frying pans so Mary could cook over the fire place.

Let us picture the little house with a fence around it and the garden. The fence was to keep the chickens, pigs and cow out of the garden. Just outside the fence and behind the house, there was a barn and other out buildings for the farm animals, and tools. Powell and Mary slipped away from the celebration early, to start their life together in the house Powell had built.

They lived their lives as the other pioneer tobacco farmers in Middlesex County. Long hours in the tobacco fields, as well as growing some corn, cotton, and a garden, tending the chickens, pigs and the family milk cow. They worked six days a week, from sun up to sun down. On Sunday mornings they went to the Parish Chapel for services. Before and after the services, they socialized with their friends and neighbors. Sunday afternoon was a time for rest and to spend with the family. On a quiet warm Sunday afternoon, Powell may have played some games with his children; or he and Mary could have just set under a shade tree and talked while the children played. This was their family time and time for rest from the long week's work.

From the Vestry Book of Christ Church Parish, we learned that the Parish paid families to keep widows and orphans in their homes. These early communities had to care for their members who became needy, for whatever reason. From the Parish Vestry Book, dated 10 October 1716: "Powell Stamper for keeping Honora Baskett 800 lb tob." And on 18 October 1717: "Powell Stamper for keeping Ditto 4 months 267 lb tob[4]." From Parish Register of Christ Church, we find where the husband of Honor Baskett died leaving her a widow. Then we find where Honor Baskett died 8 December 1720[4].

So as part of Powell and Mary's Christian and community duties they kept in their home the widows or orphans as needed.
The Parish then paid them for these services in tobacco, the tobacco was used as money in the Community.

Powell lived for nineteen years after he married Mary and they had six children that we have records of from Christ Church Parish. History shows that on the average a woman had a child every two years after they married. Since the first child we have listed was born four years after Mary and Powell were married, there could have been a miscarriage or still birth. The children were: (1) Cary born 23 June 1712, died 2 September 1720; (2) John born 1714, no record of death; (3) Susannah born 19 December 1715, no record of death; (4) Jonathan Sr. born, 21 April 1719, died 1799; (5) Letitia born 22 September 1723, no record of death; (6) Kerah born 31 March 1725, no record of death [1].

Powell Stamper died 22 May 1727, and his youngest daughter would have been only two years old at the time of his death. At the time of Powell Stamper's death an inventory of his property was made, in addition to land, house, out buildings, tobacco and money we find the following:

STAMPER FOOTPRINTS

In Will Book B, 1713 -1734 Middlesex County, Virginia, which is found in the Virginia State Library: We find Powell Stamper's inventory, 4 July 1727. "In obedience to an order of the Court held -- on June 1727, we inventorists, sworn have met and appraised the Estate of Powell Stamper, deceased, are as Follows: money in pounds, shillings and pence

8 young steers	3.10.0	Powder, shot and fish hooks	0.1.6	
3 yearlings	1.4.0	parcel of knifes and forks	0.3.0	
2 cows with calves	3.1.0	box iron and heater	0.1.3	8
barren cows	2.15.0	parcel of old books	0.3.0	1
heifer	0.15.0	47 of pewter @ 10 p/pound	1.19.2	
1 old mare	1.10.0	6a of old pewter	0.14.6	1
young mare	1.10.0	1 dish	0.2.6	
4 ewes and 6 lambs	1.13.0	1 old tankard	0.1.3	
2 old beds and		1 parcel of -------	0.2.0	
furniture	3.15.0	15 quart bottles	0.1.3	
1 bed and furniture	3.0.0	1 small looking glass	0.0.6	
1 old table	0.1.0	1 old gun	0.12.0	
1 old chest	0.5.0	1 old gun	0.2.6	
1 linen chest	0.4.0	3 pair of wool cards	0.2.6	5
old chairs	0.5.0	13 1/2 lbs. rich cotton	0.6.9	
1 felt hat	0.1.6	parcel of old cotton	0.1.0	
2 remnants of cloth	0.2.0	22a of unpicked cotton	0.3.8	
2 quires* of paper	0.1.3	8 cask of	?.?.?	1
iron p---le	?	10 3/4 lbs. of cotton @		
parcel of -----	?	4 p/lb	0.3.7	
parcel of old clothes	2.0.0	2 wedges and 1 cutting knife	0.2.6	
1 conical shifter	0.1.0	1 iron --------	?.?	
3 zaggs ?	0.1.6	2 gardening hoes	?	
1 rundlet**	0.0.7	Cask of------	1.0.0	1 -
----- iron	?.2.0	1 old tub and 3 pails	0.9.6	1
pair old boots	?.?.?	1 old rope and one old gun	0.1.?	
2 frying pans	0.3.6	3 tubs	0.1.?	
1 iron pot	0.4.0	1 sifting tray and tub	0.1.?	
1 great pot and		2 rawhides	0.2.0	
1 small pot and hook	0.12.6	cask	0.1.0	
1 ladle and fork	0.1.3	8 barren hogs	1.?.?	
1 pair --- tongs and		4 sows alive	?.?.?	
grid iron	0.1.6	1 killed sow	0.?.?	
1 brass skillet	0.2.6	13 ------ @ 12p apiece	0.13.0	
parcel of carpenters		1 pair of old shoes	0.2.6	
tools	0.13.6	1 saddle and bridle	0.12.0	

Executor: Mary Stamper (her X mark) Witnesses: J.C. Tagel, J. H. Lewis, Lawr. Orrill(*quire-book of loose pages, **rundlet - cask)

From this inventory we can learn a lot about Powell Stamper. He was not a rich man, but was comfortable for a man of his time. He farmed and owned farm animals. He grew cotton and tobacco, as well as food stuff on his farm. He did some carpenter work, even if it was only his own house and barn. He owned carpenter's tools. He could read and owned some old books, not everybody owned books at that time. Powell left his footprints in the soil where he farmed the land in Middlesex County, Virginia. He left them in the Church record books, and in the Court Records. We find that he was very much like his father John.

Mary was left a widow with five young children, Cary had died at age eight. There is a record of a Mary Stamper marrying a John Dobbs on 11 May 1735, listed in the Parish Register of Christ Church. This would have been our Mary, for at that time women did not stay widows. There were many more men than women, and men often married widows in order to get the extra land.

It would have been very hard for a woman to farm the land without the help of a man. So we will assume that Mary Brooks Stamper remarried and raised her children with a step-father.
We do not find any records where Mary and John Dobbs had any children together.

County Wilkes

Name Stamper Jonathan

Acres 208

Grant No. 456

Issued 28th October 1782

Warrant No. Entry No. 798

Entered 2 Oct 1779

Book No. 49 Page No. 162

Location On some of the head waters of little Bugabo & big Bugabo

Remarks:

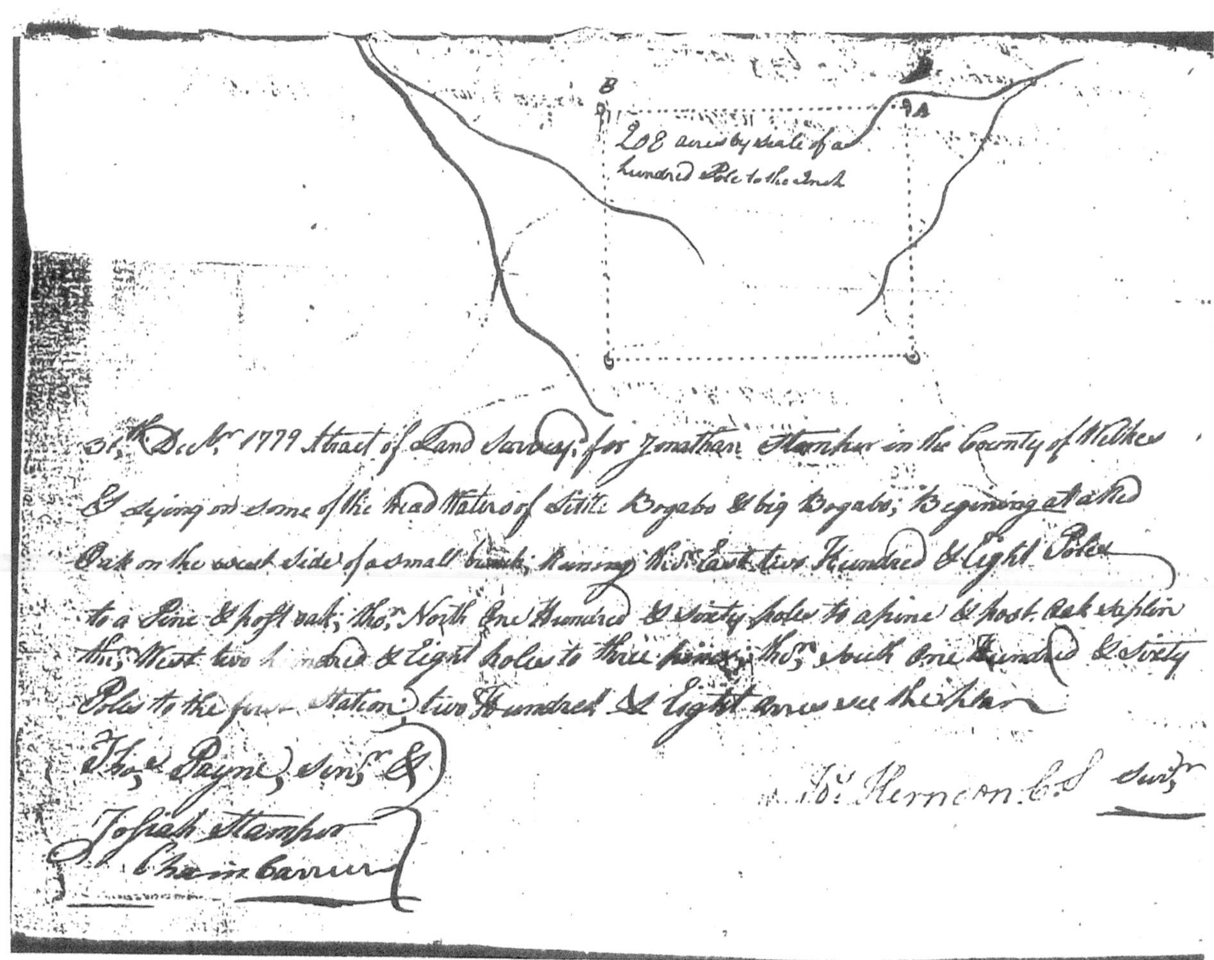

31st Decr 1779 Tract of Land Survey'd for Jonathan Stamper in the County of Wilkes & lying on some of the head Waters of little Bugabo & big Bugabo; Beginning at a W Oak on the west side of a small branch Running No East two Hundred & Eight Poles to a Pine & post oak; thence North One Hundred & Sixty poles to a pine & post Oak saplin thence West two hundred & Eight poles to three pines; thence South One Hundred & Sixty Poles to the first Station two Hundred & Eight acres see the plat

Thos Payne, Smr &
Josiah Stamper
Chain carriers

Wm. Hernon C.S. Survr

CHAPTER 3

THIRD GENERATION

JONATHAN[3] STAMPER Sr., (Powell[2]), (John[1]) the fourth child of Powell and Mary, was born 21 April 1719 in Middlesex County, Virginia. His father died when he was about eight years old[1]. We have no other records of Jonathan until we find him and his family and some other Stampers living in Amherst County, Virginia in 1763. Why he moved to Amherst County we do not know. It could have been because his father's land had gone to a step-father or another member of the family. By 1740 Middlesex County was regularly losing it's white population. Those who left were more often young married adults [3]. It seems that the Stampers were a restless mobile people with a driving urge to explore new lands looking for greener pastures. Were they looking for adventure or a better way of life? For whatever the reason we find them in Amherst County in 1763.

From Deed Book, Amherst County, Virginia, 1763, page 103. "On 7 March 1763 Jonathan Stamper bought 200 acres of land for forty pounds from John Freeman and his wife Abigail, this was on Stone House Creek, Virginia[5]"

The Stampers also owned land in Montgomery County, Virginia (at that time Montgomery County, Virginia included the Territory of Kentucky). In a book by Fothergill, "List of Montgomery County, Virginia Taxpayers 1762-1782 ", lists Isaac Stamper, James Stamper, Jonathan Stamper Sr., Jonathan Stamper Jr., and Powell Stamper, as paying taxes in Montgomery County [5].

We know that the Powell Stamper listed here could not have been Jonathan Sr.'s father as he would have been well over one hundred years old. Since pioneering has been defined as finding new and unpleasant ways of dying, he probably did not live that long. There is a record of Powell dying in Middlesex County on 22 May 1727.

Finally there is a record from Christ Church Parish in Middlesex County, Virginia that, "Powell, son of John and Sarah Stamper born 20 March 1738"[1]. That is probably the Powell listed in these tax records in Montgomery County, Virginia. The John listed here, could have been the John who was not yet of age listed in the will in chapter one, and the nephew of our first Powell. He may have been the son of Jonathan's brother who was named John, making him Jonathan Sr. nephew.

In 1767 Jonathan Sr. sold his land in Virginia and moved to what was then Rowan County, North Carolina. Surry County was formed from Rowan County in 1770 and Wilkes County was formed from Surry County in 1777. Jonathan settled on Bugaboo Creek about two miles from the present town of Ronda, North Carolina.

Jonathan Sr.'s wife was Rachel Parks, she could have been a second wife, no record of their marriage has been found. Rachel's parents were John Parks and Mary Sharp Parks[5]. The children of Jonathan Stamper Sr. that we have records for are: (1) James born 4 November 1750, died 12 March 1826; (2) Joshua born about 1753, no death date; (3) Joel Sr., born 17 May 1755, died 30 April 1833; (4) Jonathan Jr. born 1757 in Virginia, no death date; (5) Frances born about 1760, no death date; (6) Jesse born about 1765, died between 1826 and 1830. (7) Jacob born about 1762, died 15 June 1834; (8) Susannah born about 1767 no death date.

Richard and Nathaniel Stamper of Wilkes County, North Carolina, could have been the sons of Jonathan Sr. or the sons of Jonathan's son James Stamper. These Stampers lived in Wilkes County and played their part in helping form Wilkes County. At the present there are only a few Stampers living in Wilkes County. They migrated back to Wilkes County from Alleghany County. They are probably descendants of Jonathan Jr. There are still some Stampers in Alleghany and Ashe Counties, North Carolina and Grayson County, Virginia[5].

From early minutes of Wilkes County, North Carolina: Nathaniel Stamper was Constable 1806, 1807, and 1809[5].

The State of North Carolina confiscated all land in 1778. Everyone had to enter their land in order to get titles. In an early entry book of lands owned in Wilkes County, North Carolina shows: Entry 130, 8 May 1778, Jonathan Stamper Sr. entered 300 acres on Bugaboo Creek, nearly against the old Mill to Canaday's (Kennedy) line including Jonathan Jr.'s improvements. Entry 798, 6 February 1779, Jonathan Stamper Jr. entered 250 acres on Little Bugaboo Creek above Richard Allen's. An entry 799, 6 February 1779, Jonathan Stamper Sr. entered 100 acres on the water of Bugaboo Creek at the entry of his other land[5].

The above mentioned land joined Richard Allen's land. Richard Allen was a Captain in the Revolutionary War and the first Sheriff of Wilkes County, North Carolina[5].

From tax list for Wilkes County 1797: (1) Jonathan Stamper 300 acres of land and no polls (over 60 years of age). (2) Jonathan Stamper Jr., 100 acres of land, 2 polls. (3) Joel Stamper, 200 acres of land 1 poll. (4) Jesse Stamper 250 acres of land, 1 poll. (5) Jacob Stamper 322 acres of land, 1 poll[5]. At that time North Carolina had what they called a poll tax, men from the age of twenty-one to sixty had to pay the tax.

Jonathan Sr. and his sons owned enough land at Bugaboo Creek to make several large plantations. They more then likely grew tobacco the same as the Stampers had done in Middlesex County, Virginia.

These Stampers also grew some corn, wheat, and cotton. They surely would have had some cattle, pigs, sheep, and horses. Rachel, her daughters and daughters-in-law would have spun the wool from the sheep into threads to make sweaters, socks and other clothes. They spun the cotton into a cloth for dresses, shirts, underwear etc. (From an account of the sale of Jonathan Stamper Sr. estate after his death, we find that he owned a flax spinning wheel and a loom.) They would have made most of their clothes but I am sure there were also some clothes that were imported. Life beside Bugaboo Creek was not the same as it would have been beside the Piankatank River, in Middlesex County. It was much easier to get things imported from England beside the Piankatank River as ships came regularly to pick up the tobacco. We know from the will of Jonathan Sr. that he owned slaves which were needed to farm the land.

We have to use our imagination when it comes to how Jonathan Sr. and family lived. We know that farm life in those early days of our country were lots of hard labor. One thing about the farmers is they had plenty of simple food grown on the land. Their children learned at an early age that they had to work, to help farm the land. So in our mines eye we can see Jonathan Sr. his grown children, who live near by, grandchildren and a few slaves plowing the fields, picking the corn and cutting the tobacco. With Rachel and the young women cooking large meals and baking corn bread over the coals in the fire place. When the work was done in the fields and kitchen, the farm animals had to be fed and cared for and the cows milked.

On 5 March 1993 George, my husband, and I drove in search of Bugaboo Creek. It was a cool windy day, the sun was out, after a rain storm, it was a nice day to go in search of the past. I felt that I must go see the land near Bugaboo Creek. I wanted to understand what it was like to have lived and farmed there. I know that I can only imagine what it was like over two hundred years ago. When I saw the creek and meadow I felt that it had not changed much in the past two hundred years. In my mind's eye I could see Jonathan overseeing the plowing of the meadow. He left his footprints beside Bugaboo Creek. It had been a year ago that very weekend since we had visited Stamper's Landing in Middlesex County, Virginia. I thought of the contrast between the two areas. There were very large and lovely meadows already beginning to look green. These lush meadows would have been good for almost any crops or very good for pasture or hay. I was impressed.

Why the Stampers sold this good farm land and moved to the mountains, we will never know. Could it have that they just wanted to be on the move, looking for adventure? It could have been that they wanted to move to a less populated area. It appears that Jonathan Sr. bought and sold land and kept on the move, because it was an important value for him to do so.

Entries in land records indicate that Jonathan Sr. and Jonathan Jr. sold their land at Bugaboo Creek and moved to the upper Roaring River area in the 1780's.

In 1772 Jonathan Sr. served as constable in the King's service in the Parish of Jude, Surry County, North Carolina. Jonathan Sr. was a patriot in the Revolution War, furnishing horses and provisions for the Continental Army. His sons served in the Revolution War[5].

Jonathan Sr. was granted a license in 1778 to keep an Ordinary (tavern) in his dwelling house, with Richard Allen and Benjamin

Cleveland as securities[5]. I imagine the tavern was in a large front room and the family lived in the rest of the house. We can imagine they had a dart board like the ordinaries in Middlesex County, Virginia. The men of the community would come by after a hard day's work in the fields for a drink. They would relax, talk, laugh and play a game cards or darts.

Jonathan Stamper's Will Probated April Term Court 1799:

In the name of God Amen, I Jonathan Stamper Sr. of Wilkes County, North Carolina, am very old but in good health and sound memory. I give my soul back to him that gave it to me, my body to the earth to be buried. My will and desire is that all my just debts be paid. I lend all my estate and personal to my beloved wife, Rachel Stamper during her life or widowhood, I give and bequeath my son Jesse Stamper the Land and Plantation whereon I now live, one negro boy by the name of James and the bed he now lyeth on. And if the said Jesse dies without a lawful heir of his body, my will and desire is that his estate be equally divided amongst the rest of my children. My will and desire is that the negroes may not be sold out of the family.

Given from under my hand and sealed with seal and dated the Seventeenth Day of December 1793

Jonathan Stamper
signed X (his Mark)

Testator: John Forster
William Sebastian

Duly proven in open court by oath of William Sebastian
William B. Lenoir, C.C.

After Jonathan Sr.'s death in 1799, the inventory of his estate showed that he was a man of "means" or wealth.

From: WILKES COUNTY, NORTH CAROLINA
WILLS, BONDS, INVENTORIES, AND BILLS OF SALES

An account of the Sale of Jonathan Stamper Sr's Estate on the fourth and fifth of June 1799.

SOLD TO	ITEM	L	S	D
Jesse Stamper	one negro women	35	-	-
Jacob Stamper	one negro women	65	-	-
John Burton	mare and colt	32	-	-
Jesse Tollivar	one yearling colt	21	5	-
Moses Tollivar	one mare	40	-	-
William Reavis	cow and yearling	6	6	-
Rubin Parks	cow and calf	6	10	-
Jacob Stamper	one cow	7	13	-
Joel Stamper	one cow	8	-	-
Rubin Parks	cow and calf	7	15	-
John Burton	one yearling	2	17	-
" "	heifer yearling	3	6	-

Jesse Toliver	heifer yearling	3	6	-
Robert Burton	one heifer	3	10	-
George Reeves	five head of Sheep	4	5	-
David Hickerson	twenty-four hogs	17	-	-
Joel Stamper	one saddle	5	2	-
Jesse Stamper	one feather bed	15	-	-
Jacob Lyon	one feather bed	16	4	-
Jesse Stamper	pot and hooks	-	11	-
" "	oven 8/one skillet 4/ one wheel 14/	1	16	-
Jesse Alexander	one skillet	-	16	-
Jonathan Burton	frying pan	-	12	6
Jonathan Stamper	kettle	2	2	-
" "	one flax wheel	1	2	6
Jesse Stamper	pair of wedges	-	8	-
" "	one wheel	-	-	6
Jesse Tolliver	one wheel	-	2	6
Jacob Lyon	one hoe	-	14	-
Jesse Stamper	two basons	1	8	6
James Stamper	three basons	2	10	-
Jesse Stamper	eight plates	1	-	-
James Stamper	one bason	-	5	-
Jesse Stamper	one dish	-	8	6
Jacob Stamper	one pair of shears	-	6	-
Jesse Stamper	spoons	-	12	-
Jacob Lyon	one jugg	-	14	-
Jesse Stamper	one Shevel ploug	-	10	6
" "	one pair fire dogs	-	13	6
Jesse Tollivar	two axes	-	9	-
Ruben Parks	one mattock	-	8	-
James Stamper	one broad ax	-	10	-
Jonathan Stamper	one ploug	-	5	-
Jesse Stamper	ax 4/6 3 hoes 13/6 one colter 4/6	1	2	6
Jacob Lyon	one hackle	1	0	1
Jesse Stamper	one clevis	-	1	-
Ruben Parks	bar of iron	-	8	6
" "	bar of iron	-	6	6
Jesse Stamper	two flat irons	-	5	-
Jonathan Stamper	tobacco knife	-	1	-
Jesse Tollivar	one handsaw	-	12	-
Jesse Tollivar	one drawing knife	-	3	-
Jesse Stamper	one chisel	-	1	-
Ruben Parks Jr.	hammer and chissel	1	6	-
Jacob Stamper	one hymn book	-	6	-
" "	one howell	-	5	-
Jesse Alexander	one howell	-	3	-
Hezekiah Barber	one round shave	-	6	-
Jesse Alexander	one screw augar	-	11	6
George Lewis	one wimble bitt	-	3	-
Jesse Stamper	two cotton	1	12	-
Henry Johnson	one frow	-	6	-
John Burton	two cotton	-	4	7
Joseph Hammon	four pounds flax	1	0	6

Jesse Stamper	" " "	-	4	-
Willis Alexander	one augar	-	3	-
Jesse Stamper	wheat patch	-	6	-
David Hickerson	spun yarn	2	10	-
" "	spun yarn	-	13	6
George Lewis	two wool	2	10	-
James Stamper	one Bible	-	3	-
Jesse Stamper	one Testament	-	1	1
" "	one book	-	2	-
Jesse Tolivar	two books	-	3	-
George Lewis	one bottle	-	2	10
" "	one bottle	-	2	-
Jesse Tollivar	one quart pott	-	7	-
Jesse Stamper	one bee hive	-	8	-
John Burton	one bee hive	1	1	6
John Townzee	one bee hive	1	10	-
James Stamper	one bee gum	-	17	-
Moses Tollivar	one bridle	-	9	-
Jacob Stamper	one jointer	-	5	-
Ruben Parks	one jugg	-	18	9
James Stamper	one bridle	-	2	-
George Lewis	one bell	-	12	-
Joseph Hammon	two hemp	1	-	-
James Stamper	two jointers	-	5	-
John Burton	one bell	-	3	6
Jesse Stamper	one table	-	5	-
" "	two chairs	-	7	-
" "	knives and forks	-	3	-
Owen Hall	three slays 10/6			
	three butcher knives 14/	1	4	6
" "	two paper boxes and salt seller 5/			
	one file3/ two cage 2/	1	-	-
Owen Hall	two saw 1"5 one hackle 2/	1	7	-
John Burton	pair compasses	-	2	-
Jacob Lyon	one canister	-	6	-
Thomas Baker	foot addze	1	2	-
Jesse Tollivar	shoe knife	-	4	6
" "	one pewter half pint	-	3	6
Wm Raynolds	swingletrees	-	5	-
" "	one chest	-	3	-
George Lewis	hogshead 7/ Loom and slay 14	1	1	-
	Total	354	2	5

Jonathan Stamper) Adrs.
The above was retd. by Adrs. on Oath Jesse Stamper) Adrs.

The above account of sales lets us know what Jonathan Sr. owned besides the land and other things that were named in his will. From this account he had at least three slaves the two women sold here and the boy named James that he left Jesse. He had owned some books besides the Bible and Testament. Yet we are led to believe that Jonathan Sr. could not read and write because he signed his will with X his mark. Rachel may have been able to read and write.

The way I see Jonathan Stamper Sr., he was not satisfied to live in one place for very long at a time. He bought and sold several large plantations, more then likely he would do improvements and sell them for a profit. He also received several land grants. He was a hard worker, he would have to have been to farm all that land. He was a devoted family man, who's children were devoted to him as well, we can see this from his grown children moving with him. For some time he ran a tavern in his house. From his will I see he was a religious man who believed in God. Being a honest man he wanted all his debts paid.

He was a owner of slaves as were most farmers of the time, but he did care for the slaves. In his will he stated that "My will and desire is that the Negroes may not be sold out of the family." He probably could not read nor write. I came to this conclusion from the fact that his will was signed with a X. I imagine that he did his share of smoking and drinking. It is not my intention to try to judge my ancestors but to accept them as they were.

JOHN[3] **STAMPER**, (Powell[2]), (John[1]) the son of Powell and Mary Brooks Stamper was born 17 October 1714. He died the fall of 1774. His will was probated on 24 October 1774. He was Jonathan Sr.'s older brother. We find the records of his family in the record books of Christ Church in Middlesex County, Virginia. He and some members of his family lived out their lives in Middlesex county. He married Sarah Perrott on 25 March 1733. Their children were: (1) Robert born 17 December 1733, his wife name was Mildred, we do not have her maiden name. (2) John born 14 April 1737 and died 25 April 1739 this would have made him only two years and eleven days old when he died. (3) Powell named for his grandfather, this was more than likely the Powell who went to Amherst and Montgomery Counties at the same time as Jonathan Sr. We have no record of him after Montgomery County, Virginia. (4) John II born 17 August 1741, no other information. (5) Sarah born 21 December 1743, no other information. (6) Mary born 13 November 1745, no other information.

This is all the information we have of Powell's children. Records concerning his daughters are lacking, we are fortunate to follow the lines of John and Jonathan.

No. 879

County Wilkes

Name Stamper, Jonathan

Acres 200

Grant No. 826

Issued May 18, 1789

Warrant No. Entry No. 1507

Entered Aug. 2, 1782

Book No. 72 Page No. 165

Location On Roaring River: Beg at a pine under Gambrels upper line

Jonathan Stamper Plan of 200 acres of Land Laid by a Scale of Twenty Chains to the Inch

North 50 Chains — Pine — East 40 Chains — Stake — South 50 Chains — Red Oak — West 40 Chains — Stake

North Carolina Wilkes County
Surveyed for Jonathan Stamper Two
Hundred Acres of Land Lying on the
Roaring River Beginning at a Pine on
Gambrels Line Running North fifty
Chains to a Stake thence West forty
Chain to a Red Oak thence South Cross-
ing the River fifty Chains to a Stake
thence East Crossing the River to Beginning
Surveyed March 15 day 1780. Philip Jones

Benjamin Adams
Ezekiel Crankfield } C.C.

Joseph Herndon

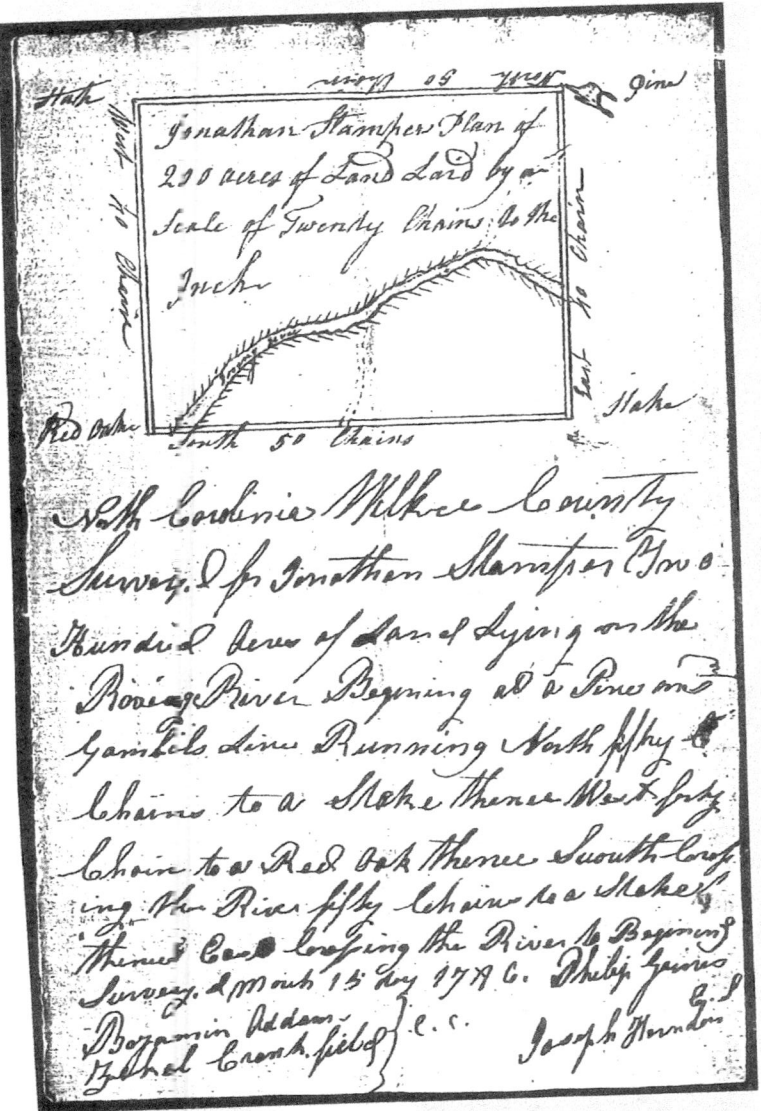

CHAPTER 4

FOURTH GENERATION

JONATHAN[4] STAMPER JR. (Jonathan Sr.[3]), (Powell[2]), (John[1]) the fourth child of Jonathan and Rachel, was born in 1757, in Virginia. His wife was Mary (Polly) Davis we do not have any information about when she was born or who her parents were. Her youngest child was born in 1800, and she died the same year. From the records we have Polly was the mother of all Jonathan Jr.'s children. He married again after Mary's death.

Jonathan Jr. bought and sold land near where his father did. They were always living in the same area until Jonathan Sr.'s death in 1799, after which he moved to what was then Ashe County, North Carolina (in 1859 that part of Ashe County became Alleghany County).

Jonathan Jr. and Mary (Polly's) children were: (1) William born about 1780, no death date; (2) Jobe born about 1783, no death date; (3) Joshua (Sr.) born about 1785, no death date; (4) John born about 1787. died about 1854; (5) Solomon (Sr.) born about 1789, no death date; (6) Susannah (Susan) born about 1791, no death date; (7) Frances born about 1795 no death date; (8) an unnamed Stamper born about 1800. The eighth child of Jonathan Jr. and Polly was believed to be Larkin Stamper bound to Joel Sr. (this Joel Sr. was Jonathan Jr.'s brother)[5].

The sons of Jonathan Stamper Sr. served in the Revolutionary War in North Carolina. Joel, Jacob, James, and Jonathan, there are pension records. Almost all able bodied men at that time saw some kind of service. Some families furnished grain, meat, hides, livestock and clothing or other goods to the Militia[5].

From land entries in deed books we can follow Jonathan Jr. as he moved from plantation to plantation. From deed book A1 page 266, "5 March 1780 grant Jonathan Stamper Jr. 314 acres on Bugaboo Creek, line between Jonathan Stamper Sr. and Andrew Canaday including Stampers improvements. In 1783 he was living on Bugaboo Creek and sold 157 acres of his land. From deed book A1, page 266, "26 July 1783, Jonathan Stamper Jr. deed to Thomas Robbins for 120 pounds of Virginia money, 157 acres on Bugaboo Creek, part of 314 acres upper tract where Jonathan Stamper Jr. formerly lived." Deed book B1 page 457, "18 May 1789, grant Jonathan Stamper Jr. 200 acres on Roaring River[5].

In 1799, after the death of his father, Jonathan Jr. moved to Ashe County. He sold his plantation at Roaring River and moved to the Cranberry section of Ashe County, that part of Ashe County later became Alleghany. It could have been that he wanted to start over in a new place, after his father's death.

Abstracts from deeds of Ashe County, North Carolina:
Entry #-1457 "31 December 1799, 200 acres on Cranberry on the north side of Turkey Knob including the good land. (John Baker marked out and Jonathan Stamper Jr. written in)." This is probably where Jonathan lived after he left Wilkes County[5].

STAMPER FOOTPRINTS

The following is a copy of Jonathan Stamper Jr.'s will, probated February Term 1831. (Ashe County, N.C. Wills, Inventors, Accounts of Guardians 1828-1842 C. R. 6. 006. 514.1, page 23).

Known all men by these present that I Jonathan Stamper of Ashe County and the State of North Carolina Being weak of body but sound and disposing Judgement, and knowing that it is appointed for men once to die, do this day make this my last will and testament in manner and form as follows in the first place I recommend that all my just debts be paid. Secondly the tract of land that I live on 300 acres my wife she is to have during her life time, also all household furniture and clothing and also what money may be on hand or owing me. She is to have support her while she lives and after that each of my children being eight alive gets one cow apiece and the remainder of my stock I want to be sold at public sale giving a reasonable credit and the money that arises therefrom to be retained in the hands of my executors for the use and support of my wife during her life. I give my son Job a certain mare and colt called Bounce and a mare called Yellow and all contracts between Job and myself concerning land is to stand good and binding on me, as the contract mentioned between us already made and at my wife's decease I want all that may remain of her property to be equally divided among my children that may then be alive and I hereby Constitute and appoint my son Job Stamper and my son-in-law John Long executors to see this my last will and testament truly performed according to the true intent and meaning thereof, and do whereof I Have hereunto set my hand and seal this 9th day of April 1822.

Jonathan Stamper (Seal)

Test
A.B. McMillan (Jurat)
Jon McMillan

(Ashe County, North Carolina Wills c. R.006; Jonathan Stamper File)

I see Jonathan Jr. to be much like his father, with a lust to wander. He was a devoted son, husband and father, who worked hard to provide for his family. He fought along with his brothers that America might be a free nation. When his family moved to Ashe County, which is in the mountains, I imagine that farming was harder and he was getting older then, so maybe his sons and sons-in-law did the heaviest work.

The Stampers of Alleghany County, North Carolina lived in the Laurel Springs, Piney Creek area and some of them lived across the state line in Grayson County, Virginia, in the Whitetop area. The Stampers living in Alleghany County, in 1860 (when the first census for the county was taken) were descendants of Jonathan Stamper Jr. born in Virginia. Jonathan Jr. left his footprints in that area of North Carolina and Virginia. I am proud to be a descendent of Jonathan Jr.

JAMES[4] STAMPER, (Jonathan Sr.[3]), (Powell[2]), (John[1]) the oldest son of Jonathan Sr. and Rachel, was born 4 November 1750, in Middlesex County, Virginia, and had moved with his family first to Amherst County, Virginia. then to Rowan County, North Carolina. His wife was Sarah Moore and from the records we have they had four children.

James and Sarah 's children were: (1) William, born 22 March 1774, died 30 April 1852, his married Emily Polly; (2) Thomas Moore, born about 1776, no death date, he married Elizabeth Stitt. We have a record of Thomas and Elizabeth having at least one son, James C. Stamper born 1812 and he married Darinda Cox. Darinda Cox was born 1814 in Kentucky[14]. Research has not proved for sure that the next two, were sons of James or younger sons of Jonathan Sr. It is believed that they were sons of James. (3) Richard, born about 1778, no other information; and (4) Nathaniel born about 1779, no other information. These two played a big part in forming Wilkes County, North Carolina. James may have had other children but these are the only ones we have a record for.

In the early entry book for land entries of Wilkes County, North Carolina: Entry 1912, no date, James Stamper entered 250 acres on the north side of Little River including all the good land near Buck Knob.

James and his family were living in Randolph County, North Carolina in 1779, the family is on the tax list for that year. In the first U.S. Census, 1790, we find James Stamper's family: U. S. Census, Randolph County, North Carolina, Hillsborough District: James Stamper (head of family)

2 white males over 16, including the head of family
1 white male under 16, and 6 white females[6]

Also from a deed dated 1807, " James Stamper of Grayson County, Virginia, 120 acres on the south fork of Roaring River including the Plantation where Jacob Stamper now lives sold to William Johnson adjustion the old Gambill line. October 1807."

James and his family moved to Kentucky. We have no record of the date they moved. There is a record of James' death 12 March 1826. In Kentucky he is buried in a Stamper cemetery beside his wife Sarah[5].

JOSHUA[4] STAMPER, Jonathan Sr.[3]), (Powell[2]), (John[1]) the second child of Jonathan and Rachel, was born about 1753. He married Jane Woodward, they had several children but we do not have a record of their names, except one of their son's was named Jonathan.

From the records of the Kentucky Historical Society we find:
(1) Jonathan, son of Joshua and Jane Stamper was a famous minister throughout Kentucky. He was a Methodist circuit rider. He also served in the war of 1812. (2) Joshua Stamper was at Boonesboro in 1779. (3) Joshua and Jane Stamper attended a sermon of Francis Asbury in 1790[5].

Joshua was a Revolutionary War solder. He lived in Kentucky, his will was probated in Clark County, Kentucky 9 July 1822[5].

JOEL[4] STAMPER, (Jonathan Sr.[3]), (Powell[2]), (John[1]) the third son of Jonathan Sr. and Rachel, was born 17 May 1755 in Virginia and died 30 April 1833. He moved with his father to Rowan County, North Carolina, (what is now Wilkes County) at the age of twelve.

From minutes of early Wilkes County, North Carolina: Joel Stamper helped to lay off road in 1803[5].

In the Early Land Entry Book Wilkes County, North Carolina: Entry 1613 on 5 February 1880 Joel Stamper entered 250 acres on the waters of Little River[5].

We see that Joel owned land near his father and his brothers. The Stampers owned a large part of what is now Wilkes County. At this time there are only a few Stampers living in the county. Joel and his family stayed in Wilkes County after Jonathan Jr. and his family moved to Ashe County.

Joel married Nancy Canady (Kennedy) on 29 July 1770. Joel and Nancy's children were: (1) Jonathan born about 1782, he married Mary Polly Sebastian 23 February 1801, in Wilkes County. (2) Nancy born about 1791, no death date, she married Charles Adams; (3) Joel Jr. born about 1791, no other information; (4) Asa born about 1790 he died 18 August 1876 in Bradley, Tennessee. He married Sarah (Betsy) Elizabeth Fender on 5 July 1821, in Surry County, North Carolina; (5) Nathaniel born about 1804, no other information; (6) James born about 1806, no information; (7) Richard born about 1796, he married Martha (Patsy) Carter; (8) Margaret (Peggy) born about 1797 married John Handy 23 December 1818; (9) Mary (Marty) born about 1798, no death date, she married Thomas Handy 24 February 1817, (10) Larkin Stamper was bound to Joel Stamper Sr. He was believed to have been Jonathan Jr. and Polly Davis Stamper's youngest, the eighth child born on 14 June 1800. Polly died in 1800. (There is more about Larkin under Jonathan Jr.'s family.)

Joel Stamper and his family as listed in the North Carolina Census: U. S. Census (the first in 1790) North Carolina, page 122.
U. S. Census 1800 Wilkes County, North Carolina, page 62
U. S. Census 1810 Wilkes County, North Carolina, page 270
U. S. Census 1820 Wilkes County, North Carolina
Male 1 over 45
Male 1 age (26-40)
Female 1 over 45
Female 1 age (10-16)
Female 1 age (16-20)
Female 1 age (26-40)
U.S. Census 1830 Wilkes County, North Carolina, no page number, list Joel Stamper and his family[6].

This information is from when Joel filed for his Revolutionary War pension. File number S-3999, issued 30 April 1833, Wilkes County,

North Carolina. Joel Stamper, stated that he was born in Amherst County, Virginia 17 May 1755, that he moved with his father to Wilkes County at the age of twelve. He also stated that he served nine months and twenty-one days in the service. He further stated that his age is seventy-seven at the time of his application on 4 February 1833.[5]. We find in Washington, D. C. in, The Daughters of the Revolution Patriot Index of 1966, on page 640, Joel Stamper is listed as being a Private in the Revolutionary War, his death date is listed as 30 April 1833[6].

FRANCES(Frankie)^4 **STAMPER** (Jonathan Sr.^{3}) (Powell^2), (John^1) the fifth child of Jonathan Sr. was born about 14 Feb 1767, died some time after 1850. She married Jesse Taliaferro whose's name was changed to Tolliver (Toliver) in 1782. Frances and Jesse had ten children.

Jesse Taliaferro was born about 1756 in Fauquier County, Virginia. His parents are believed to be Charles and Ann Kemp Taliaferro. He died at the age of eighty-two February or March 1838[7].

From 1777 to 1781 Jesse Taliaferro enlisted as a private for the Revolutionary service from Wilkes County, North Carolina. Frankie and Jesse lived in various locations in what is now Alleghany County, North Carolina. Land grants records give such descriptions as Jewel Swamp, south side of Peach Bottom Mountain, Little River, Glade Creek, and Dog Creek. They owned several farms at one time and it is believed they had slaves to help with the farming[7].

Frankie Stamper Toliver and Jesse Toliver's children were: (1) Jane born about 1783, no other information; (2) Susan born about 1785, no other information; (3) Sara born about 1787, no other information; (4) John born about 1789 no other information; (5) Allen born 18 July 1804 and died 11 February 1891, he married Susan Fender and Mahala Laswell; (6) Solomon born about 1806, no other information; (7) Martha born about 1806, no death date, she married John Fender; (8) Starling born about 1810, no death date, he married Milly Spurlin; (9) Hiram born about 1812 no other information; (10) We do not have the name of tenth child. Frankie is listed in the 1850 census as living with her son Solomon Toliver in Ashe County[7].

JESSE^4 STAMPER, (Jonathan Sr.^{3}) Powell^2), (John^1) was the sixth child of Jonathan Sr. He was born about 1760, he died between 1826 and 1830. He was probably born after the family moved to what is now Wilkes County, North Carolina. If you will remember, Jonathan Sr.'s will, he listed Jesse as the main heir when he wrote it in 1793. At that time Jesse was ill and had not yet had any children, so we could assume that he was not married at the time [5].

Records show that Jesse was a midget. We do not have a record of his height but, according to legend, he was so short he had to ride his horse to sow wheat and rye. His wife Barbara Devait was of average height. We have no information of whom her parents were. Jesse and Barbara owned a large farm.

Jesse and Barbara's, children were: (1) Jacob was born about 1795, he married Susan Claren Laurence. Some records show that there were two male children born and died before Delephia, (4) Delphia born about 1800, she was a midget, she never married, (5) Rachel born about 1802, she was also a midget, and never married, (6) Susanna born about 1805, she married Mark Shumate on 29 November 1830. (7) Clarinda (Rinda) born about 1808, she married John S. Brown 1 March 1842, (8) Sarah Ann about 1811, she married Ezekiel Brown 16 April 1844. (9) Frances I. born about 1814, she married Aaron Brown.

From the tax list of Wilkes County, N. C., 1797; Jesse Stamper 250 acres of land.

From Deed Book M, Wilkes County, N. C., 25 March 1826, Jesse Stamper, wife Barbara and son Jacob, a bill-of-sale when buying a slave.

The 1810 U. S. census of Wilkes County, N. C. list:
Jesse Stamper: 1 male over 45, 2 males under 10, 1 female 26 - 40, 3 females under 10,

The 1820 U. S. census of Wilkes County, N.C. list:
Jesse Stamper: 1 male over 45, 1 male 16 - 20, 1 female 26 - 40, 3 females under 10, 2 females 10 - 16.

The 1830 U. S. census of Wilkes County, N. C. list:
Barbara Stamper as head of house hold; 1 female 50 - 60, 1 female 5 - 10, 2 females 10 - 15, 2 females 20 - 30.
This indicates that Jesse died between 1826 and 1830, and left Barbara with a family to raise. The same census list Jacob Stamper; 1 male 20 - 30, 1 female 20 - 30, 2 females under 5.

There are deeds in 1839, Wilkes County, North Carolina where Delphia, Saryann, Rachel and Jacob Stamper deed land to John Vonny.

In my imagination I can see this little man determined to get his wheat sown, dragging the heavy bag of seeds over to his horse. How to get the bags of seeds on the horse? Use a small ladder of course. Using the same ladder he then climbed on himself and set out to sew the wheat. It was a unusual sight to watch this little man riding his horse back and forth across the field all day. He reached into the bag of seeds and threw out small handfuls of seeds into the wind. As I see it he compensated for his lack of height and did his farming like the other men of his time and place.

Jesse and Barbara raised their family and lived out their lives in Wilkes County, North Carolina. We find the family in the U. S. census and deed books. They left their footprints in the sands of time, in Wilkes County, North Carolina.

JACOB[4] STAMPER, (Jonathan Sr.[3]), (Powell[2]), (John[1]) was the seventh child of Jonathan Sr., he was born about 1762 in Amherst County, Virginia. He died in Owen County, Kentucky 15 June 1834. His wife's name was Susannah (Susan) we do not have her maiden name.

Jacob was in the Revolutionary War and fought at King's Mountain, North Carolina. Pension file # 16544 Revolutionary War, North Carolina. It has been passed down through family tradition that Jacob was a short man less then five feet. That he was a Scout and rode a horse in the Revolutionary because he was so short he could not keep up with the foot shoulders[5].

From old record books of town meetings, "Minutes of Wilkes County, North Carolina": (1) Jacob Stamper, helped to lay off road in 1803. (2) Jacob Stamper was on jury duty in 1801 and in 1807 [5].

From the Early Entry Book, listing lands in Wilkes County, North Carolina; Entry 884 26 February 1779 Jacob Stamper entered 100 acres land on the Little Elkin Branch near the Little Mountain[5].

Jacob applied for his Revolutionary War pension 1 October 1832 in Owen County, Kentucky. At the time of his application he stated, that he was born in Amherst County, Virginia, then moved to Wilkes County, North Carolina. That he joined the service at the age of sixteen.

Jacob said that on a trip to New River along the Virginia line that they captured a Tory and hanged him. (In "Draper's King's Mountain Men" page 388 he speaks of Zachariah Goss being hanged there.) Jacob was speaking of capturing and hanging Goss. Jacob stated that he was age sixty-nine at the time of the application [5].

The children we have listed for Jacob and Susannah are: (1) Jesse born about 1782 he died 16 June 1845, he married Susanna (Susan) do know her last name. (2) Jonathan born about 1784. (3) Nathaniel born about 1886. (4) Elizabeth born about 1788. (5) Nancy born about 1790.

SUSANNAH[4] STAMPER, (Jonathan Sr.[3]) (Powell[2]), (John[1]) the daughter of Jonathan Sr. was born about 1763. She married John Pleasant Burton about 1779. Susannah and John had thirteen children all born in Ashe County, North Carolina. The family all moved to Lawrence County, Indiana, except a daughter Ann, who remained in Ashe County.

Susannah and John Burton's children were: (1) Richard born about 1782, he married Nancy Edwards; (2) Martha (Patsy) born about 1784, died 1852, she married Thomas Landreth; (3) Allen born about 1786, died 1861, he married Sylvia Reeves; (4) Hutchins born about 1787, died 1869, he married Sarah Edwards; (5) John Jr. born about 1788, died 1864, he married Hannah Reeves; (6) Mary ((Polly) born about 1790, died 1864 she married Rankin Cox: (7) David born about 1792, no death date, he married Elizabeth Johnson; (8) William Buchanan born about 1794, died 1873, he married Obedience Reeves; (9) Harden born about 1798, died 1873, he married Jennie Reeves; (10) Zachariah born about 1801, died 1888, he married Ruth Holmes Core; (11) Ann born about 1803 died 1891, she married Joseph Alexander; (12) Eli (a twin) born 1807, died 1899, he married Mahala Conley; (13) Isom (a twin) born 1807, died 1885, he married Mary J. Alexander[7].

To continue the Fourth Generation let us go back to Middlesex County, Virginia, and the children of John, the son of Powell Stamper.

ROBERT[4] STAMPER, (John[3]), (Powell[2]), (John[1]) was born on 17 December 1733. He died either January or February 1808. He married Mildred --? about 1758 or 1759. Robert Stamper and his wife Mildred had ten chidden. This family lived in Middlesex County, Virginia.

The children of Robert and Mildred were; (1) John was born on 16 December 1759 and died in 1814 in Middlesex County, Virginia. No record was found of his marriage date or who he married but a record was found of his five children. (2) William we do not have birth or death dates. He moved to Granville County, North Carolina. He was a successful planter there. His will probated in the Granville County Court in 1831 named seven children. (3) Elizabeth, married John Caldwell on 27 February 1783 and moved to King and Queen County, Virginia. Most of the records for King and Queen County, Virginia were destroyed during the Civil war, and no records have been found for this family. (4) Robert, the only records in Middlesex County concerning this Robert are in his father's will. (5) Leonard was born on 14 December 1769 and he died 1820. No marriage records were found for him and it is presumed that he was never married. (6) James do not have birth date he died 1801. He married Catharine (Davis) Jackson on 20 March 1796. Catharine was the widow of John Jackson and had two daughters at the time of her marriage to James. They had a son George and a daughter Polly. (7) Sarah (Sally) we have no birth or death date, she married William Nelson Kidd on 18 May 1793. They sold their land in Middlesex County, Virginia and no records have been found for them after that. (8) Samuel was born on 6 October 1775 and died in 1818. He married Sarah (Sally) Kidd on 14 April 1801. We do not have a record of their children. (9) George born on 22 July 1777, no other information. (10) Nelson no birth date he died in 1817. He married Elizabeth Meacham on 18 January 1803 and the only known child was Frances. Elizabeth was the daughter of Lawrence Meacham and Frances Batchelor Meacham. There was no will nor estate records for Nelson.

In the (1810 Tax List of Virginia, Nelson Stamper's age was listed between 25-45, with 2 females age 0-10, 1 female 10-16, 1 female 25-45, 1 other free person and 5 slaves. Polly Meacham, sister to Frances, was probably a member of this family[16].

POWELL[4] STAMPER, (John[3]), (Powell[2]), (John[1]) was born on 23 March 1738/39. He left Middlesex County, Virginia fairly early. In 1767, he was in Prince Edward County, Virginia serving as a constable. There are no Stamper deeds, wills or estate records in Prince Edward County. It is believed that this is the Powell Stamper who was in Montgomery County, Virginia in 1782.

We do not have a record of Powell's wife. Here are the children believed to be Powell's but not proven. (1) Daniel, who married Sally Griffith on 27 December 1787, in Prince Edward County, Virginia. Sally Griffith was the daughter of William Griffith, who was surety for the marriage bond, (2) John Stamper who married Jane Chandler on 21 July 1792, in Granville, North Carolina. At the time of their marriage William Stamper was bondman and W. Norwood was the witness. Jane was the daughter of Joel and Jennie Chandler.

About the above John Stamper, the son of Powell Stamper, who was the grandson of the first Powell, it is believed that this John Stamper was the one who witnessed a deed for John Craig on 8 June 1779, in Spotsylvania County, Virginia. There were no Stamper deeds, wills, or estate records in Spotsylvania County, but tax records show a John Stamper in 1783 and 1784. After that time, he disappeared from the Spotsylvania records[16].

In September 1784, it is believed the same John Stamper appeared in Granville County, North Carolina. A John Stamper witnessed a will of Richard Henderson that same year. On 22 September 1789, John Stamper witnessed a Deed of Trust between Baxter Davis of Mecklenburg County, Virginia to John Green of Prince Edward County, Virginia. John purchased land in Greenville County, North Carolina and became a constable there. John was in Granville County in 1831 and was one of the buyers at the estate of William Stamper. No will, or estate papers were found for John in Granville County, North Carolina[16].

JOHN[4] STAMPER, (John[3]), (Powell[2]), (John[1]) was born on 17 August 1741, in Middlesex county, Virginia and died in 1774, in Halifax County, North Carolina. He married Elizabeth --? we do not have her maiden name. John Stamper and Elizabeth had four children which were named when the inventory of John's personal estate, probated in May 1774, Elizabeth, his wife was the executrix. The children named were (1) Frances, who married a Brown. (2) Robert, (3) John, and (4) Sarah[16].

$50 Reward!

I WILL PAY the above reward for the apprehension and delivery to me at Statesville, N. C., of MILTON STAMPER, charged with the murder of one Waggoner, in Alleghany county, who escaped the jail of Iredell county on the night of Sunday, December 19th, 1875; or I will pay

$25 REWARD

for his apprehension and confinement in any jail where his delivery to justice can be assured.

Description.—Said Stamper is about 28 years old, 5 feet 10 inches high, weighs 160 pounds, has black hair, dark complexion, and has a scar on one side of th face extending from cheek bone to near the mouth, and when he left had mustache and chin beard or goatee.

T. A. WATTS,
Sheriff of Iredell County.

January [illegible] 47[illegible]

CHAPTER 5

FIFTH GENERATION

JOHN[5] STAMPER, (Jonathan Jr.[4]) (Jonathan Sr.[3]) (Powell[2]), (John[1]) the fourth child of Jonathan Jr. and Mary (Polly) Davis he was born about 1786 in Wilkes County, North Carolina. The family moved to Ashe County in 1799, John would have been around thirteen years old. Ashe County is a mountainous county. When one stands on a mountain top and look over, a sea of blue mountains can be seen, the rounded tops of these maintains looks like waves on the ocean. The beauty of these mountains is beyond description, but the farming of them is nothing but hard work. I can see in my minds eye a skinny thirteen year old boy with light brown hair and blue eyes, hoeing corn in the mountainous new ground along with the rest of the men and boys of Jonathan Jr.'s family.

John married Sarah (Sallie) Lewis, at this time we have no information about Sallie. John and Sallie children were: (1) Hiram H. born 10 March 1804, died 4 March 1874, he lived sixty-nine years, eleven months and twenty-four days. He married Anora (Anna) Hackler. Anna was (research shows) of Deutsche (German) decent. It has been passed down through the family that Anna could not speak English. She was the daughter of John Hackler; (2) William born about 1806, he married Nancy Wilson on 7 February 1825; (3) Eli Cleveland born about 1809. He married Susannah (Sookie) Stamper, she was his first cousin, the daughter of Solomon Stamper and Elizabeth (Betsy) Sizemore. (4) Ephraim William born about 1808, no death date, he married three times. His first wife was Lauranne Hackler, her name is listed in some places as Susanna, she was the daughter of Peter Hackler. (5) Betsy no information, except her name is mentioned in John's will. (6) Naomi she was born about 1818. She married George Stamper, who was her first cousin, he was the son of Solomon and Elizabeth (Betsy) Sizemore Stamper[17].

John and Sallie lived in Grayson County, Virginia for a period of time. Sallie may have been from Grayson County. Their sons Hiram and Ephraim both married in Grayson County, Virginia.

From Deed books at the Courthouse in Ashe County, North Carolina we find where John Stamper received land grants totalling 300 acres, in two separate grants. The grant for 100 acres was dated 1801. The grant for 200 acres was dated 5 February 1821. Both of these tracts of land were in the Cranberry section of what was then Ashe County and later became Alleghany County. We have discovered that many of Jonathan Stamper's descendants lived in that area.

Will of John Stamper; (Ashe County, North Carolina from Will Book E page 196.)

I, John Stamper, from the aforesaid County and State being of sound mind but considering the uncertainly of my earthly existence do make and declare this my last will and testament. 1st My executer herein after mentioned shall give my body a decent burial Suitable to the wishes of my friends and relatives and pay all funeral expenses

together with all just debts out of the first money which may come into his hands belonging to my estate.
2nd I want all of my lands where I now live sold privately if it can be sold for fifteen dollars pr acre. If it can't be sold for fifteen dollars pr acre, I want it sold at public auction to the highest bidder six months after my death. It is to be advertised and sold. One fourth of purchase money to be paid on day of sale. One half of remainder to paid in twelve months and the remainder in eighteen months with Interest from date the purchaser is to give bond and good security for the payment of said debts and the land is to stand good for the purchase money.
I will that my beloved wife Sarah Stamper Shall have two hundred dollars out of money my land is sold for. And Reny Sawyers my granddaughter Shall have two hundred dollars out of the said money that the Land brings. I will that my daughter Betsy Stamper Shall have one hundred dollars out of the remainder of the money that my lands is sold for. If there is any remainder is to be equally divided between my wife Sarah Stamper and my granddaughter Reny Sawyers. I have deeded to my daughter Betsy Stamper forty acres of land heretofore the land I give her and the one hundred dollars that I will her makes her equal profertien.
I will that my wife Sarah Stamper is to have one dark red cow by the name of Beggar seven years old. I will that the rest of my personal property be sold at public auction thirty days after my death and six month time all of my indebtership is to be paid out of money that my personal property is sold for and after my debts is paid if any Surplus it is to be equally divided between my wife and granddaughter Reny Sawyers. I will that wife is to have her bed that she brought to my house and one of my bed stids bed and bedclothing one large oven and small pot. I will my daughter Betsy Stamper is to have one bed stid and clothing that is up in the loft, and a large wash pot. I will that my granddaughter Reny Sawyers is to have one bed stid known as the Zestormeal bed stid. The rest of my household and kitchen furniture to be sold at public auction, thirty day after my death. I will that my wife have one years support out of the growing crop that is now on the land is may be at my death and the remainder sold. I will that if I pass away before the present crop is made that my yoke of Cattle shall be left on the place until the crop is made then to be sold.

I hereby constitute and appoint my trusty friend J.E. Gambill my lawful exs to all intents and purposes to execute this my last will and testament according to the time intend and meaning of the same and every part and clause thereof hereby revoking any declaring utterly void all other wills and testaments heretofore by me made. In witness whereof I the said John Stamper do hereunto set my hand and seal this 5th day of Feby. 1890.

his
John X Stamper
mark

Witness S. Pugh
John M. Pierce

I wish I could know more about John Stamper. From the court records we have been able to find and his will, we can see he owned at least 300 acres of land and that he was a farmer. When he made his will, his other children not named must have had land of their own. Some of his sons lived in the same part of the county, as he did.

WILLIAM[5] STAMPER, (Jonathan Jr.[4]), (Jonathan Sr.[3]), (Powell[2]), (John[1]) the first child or Jonathan Jr., was born about 1780, in what is now Wilkes County, North Carolina. He married Peggy (probably Margaret) Baldwin, the daughter of Jacob Baldwin. William and his family lived in Ashe County, he could have moved there when his father Jonathan Jr. did.

The children of William and Peggy from the Ashe County, North Carolina census of 1850: (1) Polly born about 1804, no death date, she married someone who's surname was Austin, no other information; (2) Franky born about 1806, no death date, she married John Cox; (3) Jonathan born 16 april 1807, no death date, he married Cynthia Jones on 7 February 1839; (4) William Jr. born about 1808, no death date, he married Jane we do not have her last name; (5) Riley born about 1810, no death date, he married Nancy Cox; (6) Solomon born about 1814, no death date, his wife's name was Jane we do not have her last name; (7) Will Ben born about 1814, no other information; (8) Milt born about 1818, no other information; (10) Hiram Taylor, was born 1 September 1826, in Ashe County, North Carolina, died 23 July 1898, he married three times. There may have been other children[5].

Abstracts of deeds from Ashe County, North Carolina deed books; (1) Book C page 369 Grant number 559, 1804 the State to William Stamper 100 acres on George Lewis' line. (2) Book S page 457, 1849 fifty acres Dobson sold to William Stamper land on Peak Creek, Stamper of Ashe County and Dobson of Surry County, the land on the Cox line[5].

JOBE[5] STAMPER, (Jonathan Jr.[4]), (Jonathan Sr.[3]), (Powell[2]), (John[1]) was the second child of Jonathan Jr, born about 1781 died about 1860, he married Elizabeth (Betty) Rose. They lived in the part of Ashe County, North Carolina that is now Alleghany County.

Jobe and Betty's children were; (1) Phoebe born about 1813 in Ashe County, North Carolina, died 15 September 1901, she married Calvin Wyatt; (2) Solomon S, born about 1822, died 16 May 1901, he married Lydia Pruitt; (3) Susan born about 1823, died about 1907, no other information. (4) Jonathan born about 1828, no death date, he married Matilda Osborne; (5) Frances (Franky) born about 1831, no death date, she married Levi Cornet; (6) Mary (Polly) born about 1835, died about 1905, she married John A. Osborne in 1849; there may have a son Jobe as named is Jobe's will[5].

Abstracts of deeds of Ashe County, North Carolina: Book E page 205, 1813, grant # 1100- State to Jobe Stamper 50 acres on Cranberry. Book F page 206, 1814 grant # 1099 250 acres of land on Meadow of Cranberry to Jobe Stamper. We have from this information that Jobe Stamper lived in the Cranberry section of Ashe County. That area is mountainous and very beautiful.

From U. S. Census Ashe County, North Carolina, 1850, page 15 line 11, Family 293:

Jobe Stamper 64, head of household
Elizabeth 48, house wife
Susannah 25, daughter
Jonathan 23, son
Polly 18, daughter[6]

JOSHUA[5] STAMPER, (Jonathan Jr.[4]), (Jonathan Sr.[3]), (Powell[2]), (John[1]) was the third child of Jonathan Jr. and Mary (Polly) Davis Stamper. He was born in about 1775, in what is now Wilkes County, North Carolina. He died about 1850 in Ashe County, North Carolina. Joshua Stamper married Mary (Polly) Blevins and they had twelve children. It appears that they lived their married life in Ashe County.

From research done by Colonel Lynn B. Moore, 25 May 1991: BP 166 NSDAR "DAR Patriot Index" Washington, D. C. 1966 page 640. "Stamper, Joshua, b.c. 1760, d.a.1850, married Mary Blevins. He was a Private, who served in Virginia.

Joshua and Mary"s children were: (1) Abba was born and died about 1808. (2) Mahala was born about 1810 and died 1810. (3) John was born 1810 in Ashe County, North Carolina, do not have death date. He is buried in Stamper Cemetery, Chestnut Hill, Ashe County, North Carolina. He married Rebecca Hash first, and second Sirena Laren Hash. (4) Richard was born about 1814 in Grayson County, Virginia. His wife was named Mary we do not have her maiden name. (5) Susan was born about 1816, she married Benjamin Dawson. (6) Jean (Jannie) was born about 1818. She had a son Mattison (Bad Mat) Stamper before she married George Hall. Some researchers believe that Wilburn Stamper Jean's first cousin was Bad Mat's father[17]. Wilburn was the son of Solomon and Elizabeth Sizemore Stamper. (7) Margaret Adeline she was born 3 August 1820 in Ashe County, she died 4 February 1869. She married James Phipps Hash. (8) Catherine born about 1823, she married Abraham Hash. (9) Joshua Jr. was born about 1825, he married Susannah Hash. (10) Tobias born about 1827, he married Rebecca Rutherford. (11) Joseph was born 1828, he married Malinda Phipps. This family moved to Kentucky. Joseph is buried in Ball Creak, Knott County, Kentucky. His second wife was named Sarah Taylor. (12) Rausa Rose she was born in 1833 in Ashe County, North Carolina. She married James (Bucky) McMillan.

SOLOMON[5] STAMPER, (Jonathan Jr.[4]), (Jonathan Sr.[3]), (Powell[2]), (John[1]) was the fifth son of Jonathan Jr. he was born about 1788 and died 21 October 1854. Solomon was a Baptist Minister. He married Elizabeth (Betsy) Sizemore who was the daughter of George Edward Sizemore and Mary Jackson, and George was the son of Edward 'Old Ned' Sizemore, a Cherokee Indian. There has been much research done on the Sizemore family. Some of the Sizemore children married into the Stamper and Blevins families.

From a book by Dr. A.B. Cox, ("Foot Prints on the Sands of Time; A History of Southwestern and Northwestern North Carolina"); we find where he wrote about Solomon Stamper. "Elder Solomon Stamper of Cranberry, a Baptist minister, inclined to be eccentric and humorous, sound in doctrine, fervent in spirit, honored and respected, served his generation faithfully....[18]."

Solomon and Elizabeth (Betsy's) children were: (1) Sara Elizabeth born about 1818, no death date, she married Christopher Thompson; (2) George born about 1818, no death date, he married Naomi Stamper, she was his first cousin. (3) William born about 1820, no other information, he more then likely died as a child since there is another William in this family; (4) Jonathan B. born about 1823 no other information; (5) Riley P. born about 1825, no death date, he married Nancy Osborne; (6) Solomon Jr. born about 1817, no other information; (7) Susanna born about 1829 no death date, she married Eli Stamper her first cousin. (8) Frances born about 1831, no other information; (9) Mary (Polly) born about 1833, no other information; (10) Nancy born about 1835 no other information; (11) William born about 1837 no death date, he married Jane Baldwin; (12) Wilburn born about 1839 no other information. This family lived in Ashe County, North Carolina and Grayson County, Va.

SUSANNAH (SUSAN)[5] **STAMPER**, (Jonathan Jr.[4]), (Jonathan Sr.[3]), (Powell[2]), (John[1]) was the sixth child of Jonathan Jr. she was born about 1759, no death date. She married John Long who could have been the brother of Tobias Long, who married her sister, Frances. John Long's father was John Long Sr.

Susan and John Long have many descents living in what is now Alleghany and Ashe Counties, North Carolina. We believed they lived in the part of Ashe County that is now Alleghany County. We have not done any serious research on the Long Family though we do have a long list of their descendants.

Susan and John Long's children were, we are not sure of the dates of birth as we have found conflicting dates so I will not list the dates I am not sure of: (1) Leah born 5 May ____, died 13 July 1862, she married John Jones Jr. in Grayson County, Virginia; (2) Ellender, married Daniel Jones; (3) Mary (Polly), married Samuel Cox; (4) Washington, married Matilda Wood; (5) John R. born 16 September _____, died 22 September 1896, he married Mary (Polly) Absher; (6) Solomon, married Nancy Absher; (7) Jefferson, married Bettie Woodie; (8) Levi, married Pattie Jones; (9) Thomas no information; (10) Joshua no information[5]&[7].

FRANCES[5] **STAMPER**, (Jonathan Jr [4]), (Jonathan Sr.[3]), (Powell[2]), (John[1]) was the seventh child of Jonathan Jr. she was born about 1789 no death date, she married Tobias Long. The only records we have on them were that they had at least one child named Susan Long and she married Joshua Sturgill about 1830.

LARKIN[5] **STAMPER**, (Jonathan Jr.[4]), (Jonathan Sr.[3]), (Powell[2]), (John[1]) is believed to be the eighth child of Jonathan Jr. and Polly

Davis Stamper. Larkin was bound to Joel Sr. (this Joel Sr. was the brother of Jonathan Jr.) Larkin Stamper was born 14 June 1800 and Mary (Polly), his mother? died in 1800. Jonathan Jr. more then likely gave Larkin to Joel's family after Polly died. Larkin was probably named for Larkin Cleveland, Revolutionary solder, who was the brother of the famous Ben Cleveland of the battle of King's Mountain. Larkin Cleveland and the Stampers were neighbors and served in the Revolutionary War together. There were no other Stampers named Larkin[5].

Larkin married Emily Maupin, she was born 22 January 1799 and died 1880, she was the daughter of Thomas Maupin and Elizabeth Machie Maupin.

Larkin and Emily had seven children, they were: (1) Elizabeth born 13 March 1826 and died 18 May 1864; (2) Mariah born about 1828; (3) Joel born about 1830; (4) Marchie born about 1832; (5) Susan born about 1834; (6) Ann born about 1836; (7) John born about 1838[5].

From Wilkes County Quarter Sessions Court minutes February 4 1807: "Larkin Stamper bound to Joel Stamper, he was age six years fourteenth of last June."

JESSE[5] STAMPER, (Jacob.[4]), (Jonathan Sr.[3]), (Powell[2]), (John[1]) was the son of Jacob and Susannah (Susan), we do not have her maiden name. He was born about 1782 and died 1845. Jesse married twice, first to Nancy Sebastian, the daughter of Benjamin Sebastian of Wilkes County, North Carolina. Jesse and Nancy had eight children. His second wife was Mary (Polly) Hammond, the daughter of John Hammond. Jesse and Polly were married on 16 June 1823. Jesse and Polly had nine children [5].

Jesse and Nancy's children were: (1) Nathaniel born about 1802, died 10 July 1882, he married Sarah (Sally) Joines, 15 September 1823; (2) Benjamin born 1804, no death date, he married Susan no maiden name; (3) Joshua born 1809 died about 1880, he married Lavinia Clifton 3 December 1826; (4) Hiram born 8 April 1812, he married Sally (Sarah) Cobb; (5) Nancy born 1816, no death date, she married Elisha Cobb; (6) Elizabeth born 1818, no death date, she married William Morgan; (7) John born about 1820, no death date, he married Rhoda Jane Holbrook, 4 September 1847; (8) J. Franklin born 1822, died September 1852.

Jesse and Mary (Polly's) children were: (1) Susan born about 1824, no death date, she married Amos Gross; (2) George Riley born about 1826, died 1865, he married Mary no maiden name; (3) Mary (Polly), born about 1828, no death date, she married William Long; (4) Margaret born about 1830, no death date, she married Bennet Williams on 7 June 1849; (5) Martha born about 1833, no other information; (6) Eliza Jane born about 1835, no death date, she married William Gross; (7) David C. born about 1838, died before 1865, he married Ann Mason; (8) Sarah born about 1840, no other information; (9) Hugh born about 1843.

In the early land entry book in Wilkes County, North Carolina: Deed Book page 342, "Grant to Jesse Stamper 30 November 1801, 100 acres on both sides of south fork of Roaring River adjacent to Jonathan Stamper's line[5]".

From minutes of early Wilkes County, North Carolina: (1) Jesse Stamper was Constable 1807-1808; (2) Jesse Stamper helped to lay off road from Jesse's house on the south fork of Roaring River to Elk Spur at John Wheatley's.

Jesse and his family were not found in the North Carolina census after 1820. His family moved to Owen County, Kentucky some time after 1820. That is where Jesse lived out the rest of his life.

Will of Jesse Stamper, From Will Book C, page 285, Owen County, Kentucky.

I Jesse Stamper this day in a very low state of health, yet in proper mind do make this my last will and testament:

First I want as much of my property sold as can best to be spared to pay all my just debts. And my will is that my wife Marry Stamper have the land, the plantation she now lives on during her life time or widowhood and raise the children, and to have control of all the property belonging to the estate after all my just debts are paid. My will is that my son Wesley Stamper have the property he now claims to wit: one mare and colt, and one suckling steer. I want the other two boys to have a horse worth forty dollars each and the girls to have one bed and furniture and one cow each, this they are to have before my first wife's children get anything. After this the law makes equal division for alike, by the younger children to get this as they come of age. And I also appoint my son Hiram Stamper as my trustee to sell the property and pay my debts and no further. Given under my hand and seal as witness 18 June 1844.

In Presence of; Andrew Gross
Samuel Poe

signed
Jesse Stamper

AB. I also appoint my son Hiram Stamper to see to and give the young children their part as they come of age.

MARTHA[5] TOLLIVER, (FRANCES (Frankie)[4] **STAMPER**), Jonathan Sr.[3]), (Powell[2]), (John[1]) was the seventh child of Frankie Stamper Toliver and Jesse Toliver. She was born about 1808. She married John Fender, born 7 June 1817. His parents were Andrew Fender and Elizabeth (Betsy) Sarah Bass.

The children we have information on for Martha Toliver Fender and John Fender are: (1) Martha born 13 February 1836 in Ashe County, North Carolina, died 3 November 1897. She married Captain William Thomas Choate 3 April 1851. (2) Margaret (Peggy) born 15 April 1837 in Ashe County, North Carolina. She married Joshua Sabert Choate 19

September 1854. (3) Isom Fender born 25 May 1848 in Ashe County, North Carolina. He married Phoebe Cheek 1 October 1867[7].

CHAPTER 6

SIXTH GENERATION

HIRAM H.[6] STAMPER, (John[5]), (Jonathan Jr.[4]), Jonathan Sr.[3]), (Powell[2]), (John[1]) was the oldest son of John and Sallie Lewis Stamper. He was born 10 March 1804, in either what is now Alleghany County, North Carolina or Grayson County, Virginia. He died 4 March 1833, he lived sixty-nine years, eleven months and 24 days. He married Anora (Anna) Hackler, in Grayson County, Virginia on 2 May 1833. The marriage bond was posted in Grayson County, Virginia on 2 May 1833, Ephraim Stamper as surety. The marriage ceremony was the same day performed by Rev. Jonathan Thomas[9]. Anna was of Deutsche (German) decent and could not speak English, it has been said that all she could say in English was "Son of a bitch"[2]. She was the daughter of John Hackler. She was born on 25 October 1810 and she died 25 December 1898. Her family lived in Grayson County, Virginia. Grayson County is just across the state line from Alleghany Country, North Carolina. Since Anna never learned to speak English, Hiram must have learned enough German for them to communicate. Their children would have been able to speak and understand some of both English and German because they grew up with both language in the home. The next generation would lose the German.

At the time of Hiram and Anna's marriage there was a church in the Flat Ridge area of Grayson County, Virginia, where services were held in German. After a few generations the young people no longer spoke German and the services were stopped[17].

Hiram and Anna's children were: (1) William (Preston) born about 1834, he was married but we do not have his wife's name. We do have records that he had five children. He was in the Confederate Army and was a private of Company F, Fourth Regiment of Stonewall Jackson's Brigade, enlisted 24 April 1861, it is believed he was killed in the war[17]. (2) John born about 1836, no other information. (3) Harvey G. born about 1836 no other information. (4) Troy born 20 April 1839 and died 1 September 1900. He was married at least two times, to Charlotte Wagoner Hoppers and Median Pruitt. Records show he joined the Confederate Army the same day as his brother William Preston, and that he was wounded[17]. (5) Martha Jane born about 1840, no death date, she married John Johnson. (6) Linville Stamper born about 1842, on other information; (7) Permelia Stamper born 25 November 1843 and died 25 March 1918, she married William Hall. (8) Caroline born about 1846, no death date, we have that she married Albert Shepherd and Henry Bare. (9) Milton born 2 January 1849 and died 1 May 1884, didn't marry.

Abstracts of deeds of Ashe County, North Carolina, Book R, pages 42-43, 1845, 250 acres, Ray Adams of Calloway, sold to Hiram Stamper, land on Cranberry. Book, page 32, 1839, Jobe Stamper sold to Hiram Stamper, fifty acres for $ 75.00, at head of Meadow Creek of Cranberry[5].

From abstracts of deeds of Ashe County, North Carolina we find that Hiram had many relatives living in the Cranberry area. I will list here some of the names found from 1805 to 1858. William Stamper, Jobe Stamper, Solomon Stamper, Sarah Stamper wife of Nathaniel, Franky Stamper, Phoebe Stamper, Eli Stamper, Susannah Stamper, and John Burton, Susannah married John Burton.

U. S. Census 1850, Ashe County, North Carolina, page 514, family # 290, take 16 August 1850, copied at the National Archives in Washington, D. C. on 30 May 1992.
STAMPER, Hiram, age 47, male, farmer
" Anna, age 39 female, house wife
" Preston, age 16, male
" John H., age 14, male
" Harvey G. age 12, male
" Troy, age 11, male
" Martha J., age 10, female
" Linville, age 8, male
" Permelia, age 7, female
" Caroline, age 4, female
" Milton, age 2, male.

U. S. Census 1870, Alleghany County, North Carolina, Cranberry township; copied at the National Archives Washington, D.C. on 23 May 1992. STAMPER, Hiram, age 66, male, farmer " Anna, age 58, female house wife "Milton, age 21, male

U.S. Census 1880, Alleghany County, North Carolina, Cranberry Township; copied at the National Archives Washington, D.C. on 23 May 1992.
STAMPER, Anna, age 70, female, widow
HALL, Permelia age 34, female, daughter
" John, age 10, male, grandson
" Mary age 5, female, granddaughter.

The Hiram Stamper Planation, also known as boundaries, was in the part of Ashe County that became Alleghany County. From the abstracts of deeds we know that the plantation was at least 300 acres of mountain land. Part of that planation is now the Cowan Dairy Farm. We can imagine from what we know about how the average, family lived at that time, what life for Hiram and Anna must have been like. We know that Hiram was a farmer. He more then likely raised corn, tobacco, potatoes, and had a garden. He also had cattle, pigs, sheep, some chicken, mules and horses.

The family raised most of what they needed on the farm, after they sold the crops, they were able to buy the other things they needed. Some of the things they needed to buy was salt, sugar, and spices, shoes and ready made clothes.

The land is very hilly and the farming was not easy, and the life of the mountain people was not an easy one. Everyone in the family had to work, even the small children had chores to do. In the summer the women and children who were not working in the fields, picked wild blueberries and blackberries. With part of the berries a cobbler pie was made right away for desert that night. The rest of the berries were either made into jellies and jams or canned to use the next winter for cobblers. Vegetables from the garden that was not eaten in the summer were canned, some fruits and vegetables were dried, to eat in the winter.

In the fall they would kill a couple of pigs and a yearling steer. The meat was made into sausage, salt cured, some of the beef was dried to make beef jerky. In late winter and early spring before the garden was planted, their diet consisted of potatoes, dried beans cooked with salt pork and corn bread. They felt lucky on the nights that Anna made dried apple pies for desert. Also in the fall and winter the men and boys would go hunting for wild turkeys, deer and rabbits to give some variety to their diet.

There were three or four old apple trees out back of the house. The apples were picked in the fall and some were put in the root cellar with the potatoes. Some were dried so Anna could make dried apple pies that winter. The children had eaten some of the apples while they were still green, and had a stomach ache afterwards.

There were some chickens for eggs, the children gathered the eggs in the afternoon. On the Sunday the preacher came to dinner they will kill a chicken and make a chicken pie or big pot of chicken and dumpling.

This was the time before indoor plumbing, there was an outhouse instead of a bath room. The lighting for the house was homemade candles or coal oil lamps. The water had to be carried from the spring, for cooking, washing dishes and the jars used for canning, and of course they had to have water carried for bathing. The children were the ones who usually carried all that water. In the summer the women would wash the clothes down by the spring. They would build a fire and set a big black pot over it. The pot looked like the pot we imagine witches using, this pot was used to heat water.

Winter was the worst time, of all to wash clothes, the clothes would freeze to Anna and the girls' hands as they hung them on the line.

There was good timber on the land and as new land was needed for crops, the timber was cut and sold for lumber. Today the hills that are not used for pastures are planted in Christmas trees.

There was wood to be cut to heat the house and cook with. The house had a fireplace at each end, used for heat and cooking. The house that Hiram and Anna lived in was not much different then the house Powell and Mary lived in. The difference was the location Powell and Mary lived on flat ground beside a large river and Hiram and Anna lived in the mountains near a spring branch.

They may have had their mail delivered by a carrier on horse back, or the children may have walked to the post office. One of the earliest post offices in what is now Alleghany was in the Cranberry Community. The Stampers that stayed in Wilkes County or the Stampers who had gone to Kentucky might have written. The post office was established in 1839, in what was then Ashe County[7].

There was a school building in the community, made of logs, with one or two logs left out for air and light. The floor of the cabin was dirt, the benches were split chestnut logs[7]. In late fall after all the crops were in, despite the hardship of the cold and snow, the Stamper children went to school there. Four months of the coldest part of the year when no farming was being done is when they went to school. The teacher tried to convey some knowledge from the Blue-Backed Speller, of writing, reading, some simple math and geography. The children learned enough to get by, so they could read and write a little.

Their life was not all work and no play they would get together with some of the neighbors on Saturday night and dance to music of the fiddle and banjo. Anna and the girls would get together with other women in the area and do quilting, which was a social gathering that served a purpose. On Sunday morning Anna would have the children in their Sunday best and Hiram would hitch the horses to the wagon and everyone would pile in to go to church. We have reason to believe they went to church on Sunday morning. As early as 1849 there was a Primitive Baptist Church in the community[7]. Today there are still some Primitive Baptist in the family.

There have been no records found to show that Hiram and Anna owned any slaves to help with the work. They lived at the time of the Civil War. At least two of their sons were in the war, one was killed and another was wounded. The one that was wounded was my great grandfather Troy.

While doing the research on the Stamper family I learned of a small Stamper graveyard on what is now Cowan dairy farm, on North Carolina state road #113 near Laurel Springs, and a few miles from the Blue Ridge Parkway.

The first time my husband, George, and I visited the grave yard it was a very cold windy March afternoon. We were dressed warm and had on shoes for walking. When I spoke to Mrs. Cowan on the phone to ask if we could visit the graves, she told me to be prepared to climb a hill to see the graves. When we saw the hill I knew I was not prepared to climb it but I was determined to see the graves of my great, great, grandparents, so we started up the hill. I was excited about seeing the graves, and the extra adrenalin helped me to make it to the top. The side of the hill we went up was almost straight up. We later learned that there was a less steep side to the hill. I fell down one time and George laughed. He told me to hurry and get up before I rolled all the way back down. It was funny, I could imagine rolling down the hill. When we finally got to the top we found six graves inside a little old fence. The fence had been put up several years earlier by Dr. Clifford Stamper. The graves were covered with some of the weeds and found all the graves, two of the stones had fallen over and two of the stones were broken. The graves were Hiram's, Anna's, their son Milton's their son Troy's, who was my great grandfather, Permelia's and her son John Hall's. We cleared the grass away enough for me to take some pictures. It was too cold to do any thing else that day.

I feel as I know Hiram and Anna I have visited where they lived and raised their family. I stood on the mountain top beside their graves and looked over the boundaries of their land. As I stood there beside the graves of my great, great, grandparents and looked out over the hills a cold March wind blew across my face and all at once I felt a warm glow as their spirits touched mine. I looked out over the rolling hills from this mountain top and saw the foot prints of Hiram and Anna.

The next summer 7 June 1992, George, our son David, my sister Shirley and I went back and cleaned off the graves. George and David set up the fallen stones and fixed them so they would not fall again. Shirley and I plan to go each summer and clean off the graves.

THE HIRAM STAMPER FAMILY GRAVEYARD
NEAR LAUREL SPRINGS, NORTH CAROLINA

GRAVES OF ANNA HACKLER STAMPER AND HIRAM STAMPER

ANNA HACKLER STAMPER WIFE OF HIRAM STAMPER
(25 October 1810 - 25 December 1898)

WILLIAM H.[6] STAMPER, (John[5]), (Jonathan Jr.[4]), (Jonathan Sr.[3]), (Powell[2]), (John[1]) was the second son of John and Sarah (Sallie) Lewis Stamper, he was born about 1805. He married Nancy Wilson 7 February 1825. They lived in either Ashe County, North Carolina or Grayson County, Virginia. In 1850 they were living in Ashe County.

Listed in the U. S. census 1850, Ashe County, North Carolina:
William H. Stamper, male age 41
Nancy Stamper, female, age 31
Henry Stamper, male, age 11
Granville Stamper, male, age 9
Sarah Stamper, female, age 7
Polly Stamper, female, age 3
Cleveland Stamper, male, age 2

The information of William H. and Nancy Wilson Stamper was furnished by James J. Stamper of Independence, Virginia.

ELI CLEVELAND[6] STAMPER, (John[5]), (Jonathan Jr.[4]), (Jonathan Sr.[3]), (Powell[2]), (John[1]) was the third son of John and Sarah (Sallie) Lewis Stamper he was born about 1809. He married Sarah (Sookie) Stamper, she was his first cousin, the daughter of Solomon Stamper and Elizabeth (Betsy) Sizemore Stamper. Betsy was the daughter of George Edward Sizemore, who was the son of Edward 'Old Ned' Sizemore who was Cherokee Indian.

Eli and Sarah (Sookie) Stamper had seven children: (1) Sarah born about 1833, she married Wesley W. Brown 27 March 1852. (2) Elijah born about 1836, no other information. (3) Juliann Stamper born about 1838, she married Matthew Hart. (4) Elisha born about 1840, no other information. (5) Ira R. born about 1842, he married Joyce Blevins 14 March 1866. (6) Elizabeth born about 1844, she married Hugh Ballou. (7) Frances (Frankie) born about 1850, she married Jesse Plummer.

This family lived in the part of Ashe County that later became Alleghany.

EPHRAIM WILLIAM[6] STAMPER, (John[5]), (Jonathan Jr.[4]), (Jonathan Sr.[3]), (Powell[2]), (John[1]) was the forth son of John and Sarah (Sallie) Lewis Stamper he was born about 1812. He was married three times. His first wife was Lauranne (Susanna) Hackler, the daughter of Peter Hackler of Grayson County, Virginia. We are not sure how many of the children belonged to Susannah. Ephriam W. Stamper married second, S. J. Southhall, in Grayson County, Virginia on 6 September 1866. His third wife was Susan Ross.

The children we have listed for Ephraim, all born in Grayson County, Virginia are: (1) John G. born about 1827, (2) Julia F. born about 1829, (3) Franklin A. born about 1830, he married Elizabeth Wingate, on 28 December 1860 in Grayson County, Virginia, (4) John Granville was born 30 August 1832 in Grayson County, Virginia and died 15 October 1885 in Adair County, Missouri. He married Eliza Jane Boyd

7 September 1857, (5) Fielding R., born about 1840, died 15 September 1854 in Grayson County, Virginia, (6) Elvira born about 1844, (7) Elizabeth born about 1846, (8) William Riley born 16 June 1848 in Grayson County and died 12 January 1928 in Shuyler County Missouri, he married Sarah Grim, (9) Chaney N. born about 1849, (10) Newton Devenport born 5 September 1851 in Grayson County, Virginia and died 17 July 1875 in Adair County, Missouri, he married Ellen Marcella Lawrence 26 December 1872.

Ephraim lived, and raised his family, in the Big Ridge part of Grayson County, Virginia. In addition to farming he was a riflesmith, making rifles for the men of the county[17].

Information from James J. Stamper of Independence, Virginia states that he, James, found the graves of Ephraim and part of his family, in a family graveyard that had once been on the farm of Ephraim. In the 1950's the farm belonged to the Rush Shuler family and Mr. Shuler was 93 at that time, he had shown James the graves. The graves were marked only with field stones[17].

NAOMI^{6} STAMPER, (John^{5}), (Jonathan Jr.^{4}), (Jonathan Sr.^{3}), (Powell^{2}), (John^{1}) the daughter of John and Sarah (Sallie) Lewis Stamper was born about 1818, in either Ashe County, North Carolina or Grayson County, Virginia. She married George Stamper he was born about 1812. He was the son of Solomon and Elizabeth (Betsy) Sizemore Stamper. Naomi and George were first cousins.

Naomi and George Stamper had the following children: (1) Ludwig born about 1832, (2) Wiley born about 1832, (3) Wilborn born about 1836, (4) Mitchell born about 1840, (5) Malinda born about 1842. This is all the information we have about this family.

HIRAM TAYLOR^{6} STAMPER, (William^{5}), (Jonathan Jr.^{4}), (Jonathan Sr.^{3}), (Powell^{2}), (John^{1}) youngest child of William and Peggy Baldwin Stamper. William was the brother of John and the son of Jonathan Jr. Hiram T. was the cousin of Hiram H. written about earlier. He was born in Ashe County, North Carolina 1 September 1826. He died 23 July 1898 and is buried in Fairview Baptist Church Cemetery, Ball Grand, Cherokee County, Georgia[12].

Hiram T. married three times. Amelia (Milly) Brown she was born in Ashe County, North Carolina about 1832, died about 1865. Next he married Jemima (Mima) Osborn 13 December 1865, there were no children from this marriage, no other information.

The third and last time Hiram Taylor Stamper married Mary Burns, born 9 July 1861 in Marion County, North Carolina, and died 23 June 1934. She is buried beside Hiram T.

Hiram T. Stamper had many trades in his life time; farmer, tailor, teacher, reporter and timber hauler to name a few. He was a First Sergeant in the Confederate Army, he fought in thirty-two battles[12].

The children of Hiram T. And Amelia (Milly) Brown Stamper were: (1) Sarah Jane born about 1852, in Ashe County, North Carolina, no other information; (2) Lettie born about 1854, also in Ashe County, no other information; (3) Jesse born about 1856, also in Ashe County, no other information; (4) Wesley born about 1858 in Ashe County, no other information; (5) Mary Etta born 7 August 1864 in Ashe County, she died 24 February 1960 and is buried in the Myers Family Cemetery in Alleghany County, North Carolina.

The children of Hiram T. and Mary Burns Stamper were: (1) John Baxter born 25 April 1818 in Marion county, North Carolina, died 18 May 1978 in Marietta, Georgia. He married Martha Ann Jordan 4 March 1900, (2) Nannie (Nan) Bell born 30 January 1884 in Bryan City, North Carolina and died 26 June 1957. She married William Albert Kennedy 6 June 1906, (3) Nezzie born about 1886, she died young, (4) Alice Louisea born 30 January 1889 in Bryan City, North Carolina, died 7 May 1976. She married John Sanford Clark 20 December 1915. (5) Fred Fisher born 20 December 1893, in Bryan City, North Carolina, died 30 January 1975. He married Lula Mae Faucett, (6) Ollie Ann born 28 January 1898 in Georgia, died 17 March 1983. She married Lester Faucett.

Hiram T. was living in Bryan City, North Carolina when he married Mary Burns. They lived there until they moved to Georgia in 1894[12].

From deeds and land grants of Ashe County, North Carolina we see that Hiram T. and Hiram H. Stamper both lived in the Cranberry area of Ashe County in 1856. Book S page 410, 1856 fifteen acres Solomon Stamper sold to Hiram T. Stamper land on Peak Creek at the John Cox line and William Stamper's corner[5].

MARTHA[6] FENDER, (Martha[5]Toliver), (Frances (Frankie)[4] **STAMPER**) (Jonathan Sr.[3]Stamper) (Powell[2]Stamper), (John[1]Stamper) was the oldest child of Martha Toliver Fender and John Fender. She was the great granddaughter of Jonathan Stamper Sr. She was born 13 February 1836 in Ashe County, North Carolina, died 3 November 1897. Martha is buried in the Truitt Cemetery in Alleghany County, North Carolina. She married William Thomas Choate, he was born 29 June 1832 and he died 3 June 1864.

William Thomas Choate was a Captain in the war between the States and died of wounds received at Cold Harbor, Virginia. He is buried in Oakwood Cemetery, Richmond, Virginia. His parents were Richard (Dickie) Choate and Sarah Edwards Choate. After William's death Martha married Levi Willey[7].

Martha Fender Choate and William Thomas Choate had six children: (1) John Choate born 27 May 1852 in Alleghany County, North Carolina, died 17 June 1939, he is buried in the Sparta Cemetery Sparta, North Carolina. He married Matilda Edwards 14 June 1868. (2) Solomon Sabert born 4 July 1854 in Alleghany County, North Carolina, died 13 November 1948. He married Sarah Ann Cox 21 July 1873. (3) Sarah Jane born 22 March 1857 in Ashe County, North Carolina, died 2 April 1956. She married John H. Truitt on 12 January 1873. (4) Richard 22 March 1859 in Ashe County, died 6 March 1920. He married Rosamond (Flossie) Rector on 29 September 1878. (5) Sowell Andrew born 28 October in Alleghany county, died 3 February 1942. He married Laura Ann Edwards 9 March 1882. (6) William Thomas Jr. born in Ashe County died around 1953. He married Amelia Edwards 19 November 1888.

MARGARET (PEGGY)[6] **FENDER**, (Martha Toliver[5]Fender), (Frances (Frankie)[4] **STAMPER**), (Jonathan Sr.[3]), (Powell[3]), (John[1]) the second child of Martha Toliver Fender and John Fender was born 15 April 1837 in Ashe County, North Carolina. Margaret was the great granddaughter of Jonathan Stamper Sr. She married Joshua Sabert Choate, he was born 15 April 1833. They were married in Ashe County, on 19 September 1854. We have a record of them having two children, Nancy (Nelia) Choate and William J. Choate. They have many descendants in Allegheny County[7].

WILLIAM[6] STAMPER, (Solomon Sr.[5]), (Jonathan Jr.[4]), (Jonathan Sr.[3]), (Powell[2]), (John[1]) born about 1804 in Ashe County, North Carolina and died in Kentucky. He was a farmer. William married Jane Baldwin, daughter of Jacob Baldwin and Mary (Polly) Hays Baldwin, circa 1830 in Ashe County, North Carolina.

William and Jane had fourteen children: (1) Nathaniel, (2) Margaret, (3) Martha, (4) Eli, (5) James, (6) Polly, (7) Nancy born circa 1843 in North Carolina, (8) Mary Ellen born circa 1846 in North Carolina (The 1850, Ashe County, North Carolina census gives Ellen's age as four. The 1870, Boyd County, Kentucky census gives Mary as twenty four years old. The two names have been combined to make this record[19], (9) Emily born circa 1849 in North Carolina, (10) Jane born circa 1852 in North Carolina, (11) Rison born circa 1854 in North Carolina, (12) Rebecca born circa 1857 in North Carolina, (13) William H. born circa 1861 in North Carolina, and (14) John F. born May 1869 in Kentucky.

SOLOMON[6] STAMPER JR., (Solomon Sr.[5]), (Jonathan Jr.[4]), (Jonathan Sr.[3]), (Powell[2]), (John[1]) born about 1805 in Ashe County, North Carolina, This family went to Indiana. He married Sally--? He was a farmer. Solomon Jr and Sally had six children all born in North Carolina.

The children of Solomon Jr. and Sally Stamper were: (1) Meredith born about 1841, (2) John born about 1844, (3) Caroline born about 1846, (4) Margaret born about 1847, (5) Lutie born about 1848, and (6) William born about 1850.

After the death of Solomon Sr. in 1854 in Ashe County, North Carolina, Solomon Stamper of Greene County, Indiana gave Power of Attorney to his brother Jonathan B. Stamper to look after his interest in the estate of Solomon Sr. (from Ashe County, North Carolina Estate Records C.R. 006, 508.29; Solomon Stamper File 1854, and Ashe County Deed Book S page 243.)

JONATHAN B.^{6} STAMPER, (Solomon Sr.^{5}), (Jonathan Jr.^{4}), (Jonathan Sr^{3}), (Powell^{2}), (John^{1}) born about 1810 in Ashe County, North Carolina. He married Cynthia Jones on 7 February 1839, she may have been his second wife. He was a farmer and a Minister. This family went to Greene County, Indiana. (The Stamper Stage) Vol 1, #4 Page 93; gives the 1850 census for this family as being in Green County, Indiana.

The children we have listed for Jonathan B. Stamper are: (1) Allen born about 1832, (2) Charlotte born about 1835, (3) Martha born about 1840, (4) Reed born about 1841, (5) Mary born about 1843, (6) Macey born about 1844, (7) Jonathan born about 1847 the above listed children were born in North Carolina, (8) Elizabeth born about 1849 was born in Indiana.

JEAN (JENNIE)^{6} STAMPER, (Joshua^{5}), (Jonathan Jr.^{4}), (Jonathan Sr.^{3}), (Powell^{2}), (John^{1}) was the daughter of Joshua Stamper and Mary (Polly) Blevins Stamper. She was born about 1818, in Ashe County, North Carolina. She had a son before she was married. His name was Masterson (Bad Mat) Stamper.

Jean (Jennie) Stamper married George Hall. We do not have a record of the children she had with George Hall. We believe that she and George Hall lived in Grayson County, Virginia.

One source states that Wilborn Stamper could have been Masterson (Bad Mat's) father. Wilborn was the first cousin of Jean (Jennie) Stamper. He was the son of Solomon and Elizabeth Sizemore Stamper[17].

CHAPTER 7

SEVENTH GENERATION

TROY G/C?[7] STAMPER, (Hiram H.[6]), (John[5]), (Jonathan Jr.[4]), (Jonathan Sr.[3]) (Powell[2]), (John[1]) was the forth child of Hiram and Anna Hackler Stamper he was born on 20 April 1839, died 1 September 1900. He married at least two times. First to Charlotte (Lottie) Wagoner, she was born 20 June 1838. She was married before to Jacob Hoppers. There were some children by her first marriage but we do not have a record of how many. Elzina Hoppers was her oldest child. According to family tradition, Charlotte (Lottie) was Cherokee Indian. Lottie died 13 June 1880, and is buried in the cemetery of the Cranberry Primitive Baptist Church, off N. C. state road 1607, two and a half miles south from junction of N.C. state roads 113 and 221 on the Ashe County side.

Charlotte (Lottie)[5] Wagoner was the daughter of Henry Wagoner Junior and Charlotte[4] Sizemore Wagoner. Charlotte Sizemore was the daughter of Owen[3] Sizemore and Rebecca Anderson Sizemore. Owen Sizemore was the son of George Edward[2] Sizemore and Annie Elizabeth Hart Sizemore. Annie Elizabeth Heart was part Indian also. George Edward Sizemore was the son of Edward (Old Ned)[1] Sizemore and Elizabeth Jackson Sizemore, Elizabeth was Indian. Old Ned Sizemore was alleged to be Cherokee Indian, research shows that his wife was Cherokee Indian. Old Ned was born about 1725 in Virginia. His father could have been William, Henry, or Ephraim Sizemore. After more then twenty years of research we find that our Indian ancestor could have actually been Ned's wife. [Information from more then 20 Sizemore family researchers, Ronald L. Blevins, Archie Blevins, Ralph J. Schuler, George H. Latham and excerpts from the "Heritage of Ashe County 1799-1984"], [10].

The children we are most sure belonged to Troy and Charlotte (Lottie) together are: (1) Harry Monroe (Monroe) born in 1867, died 7 December 1947. He moved to West Virginia about 1891. He married three times all in West Virginia. He was about eighty years old when he married the last time. He and his much younger wife moved to Galax, Virginia. She was a nurse and worked in the hospital in Galax. When he died his body was brought back to Alleghany County to be buried, as this was what he had requested, (2) Hiram born about 1869, no other information, (3) Laura born 16 September 1872, died 20 February 1958, she married Fielden Caudill, they were divorced, (4) John Ander born 3 April 1874, died 12 December 1920, he married Mary Emoline Blevins. Charlotte (Lottie) Wagoner Hoppers Stamper, died 6 June 1880.

The Stampers were Confederates, when the war between the States started they were eager to volunteer, Troy was among them. Troy and his brother William Preston enlisted 24 April 1861. They were Privates of Company F, Fourth Regiment of Stonewall Jackson's Brigade (Grayson of Virginia Daredevils) - men from Elk Creek Valley, Virginia. Troy was wounded, his bother William Preston was killed.[17]

Also volunteering from the Cranberry area was Elisha Blevins. Some years later the daughter of Elisha would marry the son of Troy. Practically all men from Alleghany County of fighting age volunteered in two companies. The companies were commanded by Captain Steven Wilson and Captain J. H. Doughton CSA[7].

It has been passed down, family tradition, that Troy later joined the North, probably after his wounds had healed, from where he had been wounded. We have no documentation of his joining the North. Some rumors are that he deserted both the South and the North.

In the 1870 U. S. Census we find Troy's family living in the Cranberry Township of Alleghany County, North Carolina.

Stamper, Troy	age 30	farmer
Stamper, Lottie	age 31	house wife
Stamper, Jane	age 12	daughter
Stamper, Elizabeth	age 10	daughter
Stamper, Hiram	age 1	son.

We do not know why there is so much difference in the ages of the second and third child. It makes one wonder if the two oldest children were from still an earlier marriage. Or it could be that they were Lottie's children by her first marriage and listed as Stamper since they were all the same family. We do find in the next census 1880, Lottie has children living with her, with the name of Hopper which are not these two.

Harry (Monroe) was two years older then Hiram and we do not find him in any of the census. We can only speculate why this is. It is my guess that Monroe was staying with one of Troy's relatives when that census was taken. After talking with Monroe's granddaughter on 20 September 1993 we learned that Monroe sometimes stayed with his grandparents Hiram and Anna. Monroe's granddaughter Helen stated, "Grandpa said he could remember staying with his grandparents and his grandmother could not speak English. When he did something she did not like and she could not make him understand that she wanted him to stop, she would hit him with her cane.[13]"

The 1880 Census shows the family still living in the Cranberry Township. I copied the census at the National Archives in Washington, D. C.

U. S. Census 1880, Alleghany County, North Carolina, Cranberry Township:

Stamper, Troy	age 40		farmer
Stamper, Charlotta	age 40	Ind.	house wife
Stamper, Hiram	age 11	Ind.	son
Stamper, Louria	age 6		daughter
Stamper, Johnander	age 5		son (John Ander?)
Hoppop, Elzina	age 18		daughter (Hoppor?, Hoppers?)
Hoppop, Florence	age 9	Auft	daughter (adopted?)

From (STAMPER COURT RECORDS, MIDDLESEX COUNTY, VIRGINIA 1673-1852) page 222; list Troy G/C? Stamper as having these children: (1) W. P. Stamper (2) Robert, (3) Lonnie, (4) Cleveland, and that the family resided in Mitchell County, North Carolina.

Troy's last wife was Median Pruitt, the daughter of Joel Pruitt. Troy and Median were married in Alleghany County, North Carolina on 19 March 1881. We are not sure how many children they had together. They had a son, Grover Cleveland (Cleve) (G.C.), he was their youngest child. Cleve married Bessie Ashley on 23 December 1914 they had twelve children. From family tradition there was an Aunt Larmia, who could have been an older sister to Cleve[2].

When Lottie died Troy had several small children with the youngest being just six years old. Median was their step mother and helped to raise them. Troy and Median were married almost nineteen years before he died.

We have no record of what their life was like. It appears that Troy farmed, he could have helped Hiram with his farming. It is believed that when Hiram died he left part of the farm to Troy. It has been passed down that Troy made whisky and that he drank quite a lot of it himself. The family lived in the Cranberry area of Alleghany, when two of the U. S. Census were taken.

In 1900 Troy was sick we do not know from what. He was living with John Ander Stamper's family down in the mountain, which was in Wilkes County. He must have been sick for some time as passed down by family tradition. He was a man who did a lot of swearing and was very hard to live with, while he was sick.

We have heard from several sources that Troy was one of the meanest men in the area. It is believed that Median and Cleve were also living with John Ander's family at the time Troy was sick.

Mary, John Ander's wife was a very religious women and the swearing was almost more then she could take. It has been told that he cursed up to two weeks before he died. Mary told her children that she prayed he would hurry up and die, so she would not have to listen to his cursing.

What can I say about Troy? He was a Confederate solder. He farmed in the Cranberry Community. He was married at least two times. He had a large family with his own children and step children. When he was sick he lived with one of his older sons and was a crabby old man.

Troy died on 1 September 1900, and his body was taken up the mountain and he was buried beside his father Hiram Stamper in the family cemetery, in Cranberry Township. (See more about the cemetery named in Chapter 5.) They would have to have taken his body by horse and wagon to the cemetery and that must have been quiet a job getting up the mountain.

We have been told that Lynn Stamper, John Ander's oldest son put up the stone to mark Troy's grave. His stone is different then the rest of the family buried there.

Median lived many years after Troy died. About five years after Troy died Median went to Ashe County in answer to an ad in the newspaper from a man named Ashley. Mr. Ashley's wife was sick and he needed someone to help him care for her. Median took her youngest son, Grover Cleveland (Cleve), who was about 14 years old with her. Years later after Mrs. Ashley had died Median married Mr. Ashley. Grover Cleveland (Cleve) married Mr. Ashley's daughter, Bessie, and they had twelve children.

After Mr. Ashley died, Median later married someone from Virginia named Rowe[2].

GRAVES OF TROY STAMPER AND WIFE CHARLOTTE WAGNOR STAMPER

WILLIAM (PRESTON)^{7} STAMPER, (Hiram H.^{6}), (John^{5}), (Jonathan Jr.^{4}), (Jonathan Sr.^{3}), (Powell^{2}), (John^{1}) the oldest son of Hiram and Anna Hackler Stamper was born 1833. We do not have his wife's name. His children were: (1) J. Harvey born about 1854, (2) Chapman born about 1856, (3) Revis born about 1858, (4) Garnett born about 1860, (5) Walter born about 1861.

Preston and his brother Troy enlisted in the Confederate Army 24 April 1861. They were Privates of Company F, Fourth Regiment of Stone wall Jackson Brigade (Grayson of Virginia Daredevils). It is believed that Preston died during this war and Troy was wounded[17].

HARVEY G.^{7} STAMPER, (Hiram H.^{6}), (John^{5}), (Jonathan Jr.^{4}), (Jonathan Sr.^{3}), Powell^{2}), (John^{1}) was the third child of Hiram and Anna Hackler Stamper he was born about 1840. He married Frances (Franky) we do not have her maiden name. They had at least one son whom they named after Harvey's brother William Preston, who died in the Civil War. Their son William Preston was born about 1861. He married Almedia Shepherd 23 March 1885 in Alleghany County, North Carolina.

MARTHA JANE^{7} STAMPER, (Hiram H.^{6}), (John^{5}), (Jonathan Jr.^{4}), (Jonathan Sr.^{3}), (Powell^{2}), (John^{1}) was the fifth child of Hiram and Anna Hackler Stamper, she was born about 1844. She married John Martian Johnson 6 December 1866 in Alleghany county. They had at least one child Frances Louise born about 1860, she married Joseph Preston Holbrook.

PERMELIA^{7} STAMPER, (Hiram H.^{6}), (John^{5}), (Jonathan Jr.^{4}), (Jonathan Sr.^{3}), Powell^{2}), (John^{1}) was the sixth child of Hiram and Anna Hackler Stamper, born 25 November 1843, died 25 March 1918. She is buried beside her son John in the Stamper Cemetery. She married William Hall, no information about him. In the U. S. Census for 1870 we find William and Permelia's family living in the Cranberry area a few house holds from Hiram's.

Permelia and William's children from the 1870 census: (1) James born 1866, (2) Martha, born 1868, (3) John A., born 14 February 1870, died 23 September 1888, making him eighteen years old when he died, (4) Mary, born about 1875, no other information. From birth and marriage records at the Alleghany County courthouse we find these records: (5) Kate Hall, born 27 August 1886, mother Permelia Hall no father listed. Kate married G. W. Hoppers on 7 September 1908, in Alleghany County, North Carolina.

From the 1880 census in Alleghany County, North Carolina, Cranberry Township we find:
Stamper, Anna, age 70, a widow
Hall, Permilia age 34, daughter
Hall, John, age 10, grandson;
Hall, Mary, age 5, granddaughter.

It was told to us that all the land that belonged to Hiram and Anna Stamper got out of the Stamper family because it went to someone that Permelia married. We have not as yet searched land deeds to see if it is a true fact.

JOHN BAXTER[7] STAMPER, (Hiram T.[6]), (William[5]), (Jonathan Jr.[4]), (Jonathan Sr.[3]), (Powell[2]), (John[1]) was the oldest child of Hiram T. and Mary Burns Stamper, he was born 25 April 1881 in Bryan City, North Carolina, died 18 May 1978 at the age of ninety-seven years, in Marietta, Georgia, He married Martha Ann Jordan 4 March 1900[12].

The children of John Baxter and Martha Ann Jordan Stamper were; (1) Lila born 27 April 1904, she married Paul Grogan. They had two children. As of January 1993 she was still living. (2) Effie Lee born 13 January 1906, she married George Whitefield. They had two children. (3) Laska (Laky) born 3 November 1907, she married Roy Westbrook. They had two children. (4) Wade Edward born 27 June 1909, he married Mildred Holcomb. They had three children. (5) Hulbert Sherman born 7 December 1910, died 9 May 1980, he married Fannie Sandford. (6) Maud Ann born 29 December 1913, she married Grady York. They had two children. (7) Clyde born 8 December 1916, she married Gilbert Rogers. They had three children. (8) Reba born 22 April 1919, she married George York. They had one child[12].

SOWELL ANDREW[7] CHOATE, (Martha[6] Fender), (John[5]Fender), Frances (Frankie)[4] **STAMPER**), (Jonathan Sr.[3]), (Powell[2]), (John[1]) was the fifth child of Martha Fender Choate and Captain William Thomas Choate born 28 October 1861 in Alleghany County, North Carolina. He died 3 February 1942 and is buried in the Sparta Cemetery, Sparta, North Carolina.

Sowell married Laura Ann Edwards born 12 February 1862 in Alleghany County, North Carolina. She died 16 March 1952, and is buried in the Sparta Cemetery with her husband. Her parents were Haywood Thomas Edwards and Lucinda Carr Edwards.

Sowell was only three years old when his father Captain William Thomas Choate died of wounds received at Cold Harbor, Virginia, one of the bloodiest and hardest fought battles of the Civil War.

His mother Martha Fender Choate married Levi Willey 22 April 1875, Sowell was fourteen at the time. After his mother married she moved to another farm with her husband. It is believed that Sowell stayed on at the farm with his older brothers and sisters[7].

Sowell was a farmer dealing in cattle, horses, and breeding live stock. He was in the dry-goods business for several years with the firm of Fields and Hackler. He had two terms, from 1904 to 1908, as sheriff of Alleghany County, North Carolina.

He had little formal education other then Zion and some other county-free schools. He helped to build a school building on his land. Which was known as the Choate School. A desire for education was instilled in his children. Five of his eight children became doctors[7].

The children of Sowell Andrew Choate and Laura Ann Edwards Choate were all born in Alleghany County, North Carolina. (1) Dr.Glen William born 23 January 1883, died 1 October 1963. He married Donna Osborne 20 October 1909. They had three children: (a) Page, (b) Prue, and (c) Neil. (2) Dr. Bert Oscar born on 13 March 1885, died 10 February 1973. He married Sarah Jane (Janie) Baker on 23 June 1908, in Grahams Forge, Wythe County, Virginia. They adopted one son and had four other children: (a) Clete Barnett Choate (adopted), (b) Hugh, (c) Ray, (d) Annie Marie, and (e) Emogene. (3) Dr. James Walter born 13 March 1887, died 17 October 1977. He married Dorothy Collins 28 June 1916. They had four children: (a) James Walter Jr., (b) Kathleen, (c) Collin, and (d) William (4) Dr. Posey (Leff) born 20 December 1889, died 16 May 1961. He married Myrtle Miller Beeker 20 June 1917. Their children are : (a) Wade, (b) Thomas, (c) Charles Dean, and (d) Billy Caroll. (5) Dr. Edger Carr born 17 February 1892, died 29 May 1979. He married Selma Reeves 7 November 1919. Their children are: (a) Alice Carr, (b) Anna, (c) Joseph A. and (d) Jane Dickie. (6) Andrew Vance born 24 November 1894, died 8 October 1980. He married Rebecca Sue Osborne 22 June 1921. Rebecca was a school teacher for forty-five years, retiring in 1965 with the longest teaching record of any one in Alleghany, as of 1986. Their children are: (a) Vancine and (b) Wanda Lee. (7) Harriet (Hattie) born on 17 April 1898 still living as of 1986. She married Russell Winfred Whitener 10 August 1921. Their children are: (a) Jean and (b) Joan. (8) Annie Laurie born 6 November 1902 still living as of 1986. She married Daniel Jay Whitener 23 September 1925. They had one son Carr[7].

I have added this information about the Choate family as they were important in the history of Alleghany North Carolina. Doctors Bert and Leff were country family doctors for the county for around fifty years. Before there were cars in the county, they rode horses to make house calls on the sick and to deliver the babies of the county. They shared an office and practiced medicine in the county for over fifty years. They were descendants of Jonathan Stamper Sr. who was born in Middlesex County, Virginia, 21 April 1719.

NANCY (NALIA)^{7} CHOATE, (Margaret (Peggy)^{6} Fender), (Martha^{5} Toliver), (Frances (Frankie)^{4} **STAMPER**), (Jonathan Sr.^{3}), (Powell^{2}), (John^{1}) was the daughter of Joshua Shabret Choate and Margaret (Peggy) Fender Choate. She was the great-great granddaughter of Jonathan Stamper Sr. She was born in Alleghany County 13 November 1855 and died 6 April 1942 in Galax, Virginia.

Nancy (Nalia) Choate married Henry R. Richardson on 19 September 1871. He was born 28 May 1853 in Alleghany County and died 16 February 1920 in Galax, Virginia[7].

Henry R. Richardson and Nancy (Nalia) Choate had thirteen children: (1) Emmett Jefferson Richardson born 9 July 1872 in Grayson County, Virginia, and died 12 November 1946. He married Susannah

(Sue) Tedder 5 November 1893. (2) Margaret (Peggy) born 30 September 1873 in Alleghany County, died 20 March 1958. She married Daniel Monroe Edwards. (3) Martha Jane born 29 August 1875, died 13 February 1943. She married William Lee Stamper 9 November 1898 they moved to Dunlow, Wayne County, West Virginia. (4) Laura Etta born 3 January 1878 in Alleghany County and died 6 January 1909. She married Rufus Center Edwards. (5) Sarah Artella born 4 December 1879 in Alleghany County and died 6 November 1935. She married Mack Wagoner 28 January 1912. (6) Louella born 2 October 1881 in Alleghany County and died 2 March 1960. She married Robert Hanks 25 September 1898. (7) Sabert Alexander born 17 October 1884 died 4 May 1964. He married Emma Lou Todd 28 January 1912. (8) Clara Maye born 24 October 1886 died 15 April 1931. She married Ellis Tedder 15 April 1905. (9) Sessie born 28 November 1888 died 21 November 1965. She married Walter Blevins 13 October 1905. 10) Cora Viola born 3 April 1890 died 15 February 1981. She married Arthur Greene 10 January 1909. (11) Robert Gwyn born 28 January 1892 died 7 December 1956. (12) Hattie Virginia born 9 February 1894 died 6 May 1979. She married Arza L. Caudell on 28 March 1914. (13) Henry Ivan born 20 March 1896 died 20 March 1964. He married Fannie Smith[7].

MASTERSON (BAD MAT)[7] STAMPER, (Jean (Jennie)[6]), (Joshua[5]), (Jonathan Jr.[4]), (Jonathan Sr.[3]), (Powell[2]), (John[1]) was the illegitimate son of Jean (Jennie) Stamper, he was born in 1836, and died in 1915, he is buried in a Stamper grave yard in White Top, Virginia. His father may have been a Phipps as Masterson was listed as Madison Phipps in the 1850 census for Ashe County, North Carolina. He went by Stamper and was called (Bad Mat Stamper), some say he was called (Devil Mat). James J. Stamper of Independence, Virginia said, "My research shows that Wilborn Stamper was Masterson Stamper's father[17]".

Mat married Jane Rutherford on 4 March 1856, in Grayson County, Virginia. His age was listed as eighteen at the time of his marriage and his mother signed giving her permission for him to marry, she signed as Jean Hawl. His father was listed as unknown. Wilborn Stamper signed as a witness. Jane Rutherford was listed as being twenty years old at the time of the marriage. We have records of two children that they had; (1) Catherine born about 1857, no other information. (2) Abraham born about 1870. Abraham married Ruth Emaline, we do not have maiden name. There may have been other children.

This story told by James J. Stamper: "Mat, was often called "Devil Mat" he was so mean. One time he was not listed in the U. S. Census for Grayson County, because he was in jail in Kentucky. He told the jailer's wife such a sad story about how he wanted to get home to Virginia to see his wife and kids. She felt sorry for him, she gave him some of her clothes, he dressed up like a women and escaped. After he escaped he did go home to his wife and children, in Virginia".

CHAPTER 8

EIGHTH GENERATION

JOHN (ANDER) ANDREW[8] **STAMPER**, (Troy[7]), (Hiram H.[6]), (John[5]), (Jonathan Jr.[4]), (Jonathan Sr.[3]), (Powell[2]), (John[1]) was the son of Troy and Charlotte (Lottie) Wagoner Hoppers Stamper. He was born 3 April 1874 in Alleghany, North Carolina, he died 12 December 1920. In some records his name is listed as John Andrew, and in others it is listed as John Ander. He was called John Ander but that could have been the way the people of the mountains at that time said Andrew.

He married Mary Emoline Blevins she was born 10 August 1875 and died 18 November 1941. She was the daughter of Elisha and Nancy Adams Blevins. Elisha was born about 1830 and Nancy was born about 1839. From family tradition Nancy Adams was of German decent.

Elisha was a Private in the Civil War. He enlisted 12 December 1864 in Alleghany county from the township of Cranberry and was discharged 20 June 1865 because of a relapse of the measles.

From the U. S. Census 1880, Alleghany County, Cranberry Township, North Carolina: Mary was the youngest of seven children. She was around seven or eight years old when Nancy died. Her brothers and sisters were: (1) Celia J., (2) William, (3) John Harvey, (4) Millard Freeland, (5) Calloway, (6) Rhoda Catherine.

John would have been about six years old when his mother died. We have no record if he was raised by his stepmother Median Pruitt, or by some other family member. John had several sister and brothers as well as half brothers and sisters. There was one sister and brother he remained close to all his life, Laura and Harry Monroe.

We may never know what his life as a boy and young man was like. We do know from church records and family tradition that he was a member of the Basin Creek Baptist Church. His mother was buried in the cemetery of Cranberry Primitive Church.

From the marriage records of Alleghany County, North Carolina, we find John A. Stamper and Mary E. Blevins getting married on Valentine's day 1897 in the township of Cranberry, North Carolina. He was twenty two years old and Mary was twenty.

John and Mary were married in Alleghany County, North Carolina 14 February 1897, by John A. Richardson, J. P.. John and Mary had eight children, four boys and four girls.

Their children were: (1) Linville (Lynn) born about 1898, he married Effie Lutricia Hendrix; (2) Schley Bertie (Bert), born on 12 February 1900, he married Carrie Ann Hendrix, Effie's sister;(3) Verdie Alice (Verd), born 1 May 1902, she married James Paul Miles (4) Minnie Inez (Ine), born 16 May 1904, she married Raymond Miles, Paul's brother; (5) Onley Eugene, born 12 September 1907, . He married Elizabeth (Liza) Shaw; (6) Bacle W. (a twin), born 24 July 1912, he married Hazel Royal; (7) Macle (a twin), born 24 July 1912, she married Marshal Shore; There was a miscarriage of twins; and (8) Irene Laura born on 15 March 1920 she married two times, first to Marvin Moore, divorced and then married Steve Gilbuena.

We next find them living in Wilkes County, North Carolina. Listed here are copies from the U. S. Census.

From the 1900 U. S. Census Wilkes County, North Carolina, Walnut Grove Community, finds:
Stamper, John A., born April 1874, age 26, farmer
Stamper, Mary Blevins, born August 1875, age 25, house wife
Stamper, Linville, born November 1897, age 2, son
Stamper, Bertie, born November 1900, age 3 months, son
Stamper, Cleve, born July 1890, age 9, brother.

The Cleve listed here was Grover Cleveland Stamper, the son of Troy and Median Pruitt Stamper. He lived with John and Mary for about four years after Troy died.

U. S. Census 1910 Alleghany County, North Carolina copied from soundex at the National Archives, Washington, D.C.
Stamper, John A., age 36, farmer
Stamper Mary E, age 35, house wife
Stamper, Linville K., age 12, son
Stamper, Schley B., age 10, son
Stamper, Verdie A., age 7, daughter
Stamper, Minnie I., age 5, daughter
Stamper, Onley E., age 3, son.

U. S. Census 1920 Alleghany county, Glade Creek township;
Stamper, John A., age 45, white, can read and write, owns farm.
Stamper, Mary E., age 44, house wife can read and write.
Stamper, Onley E., age 12, son, attended school that year.
Stamper, Bacle, age 7, son, attended school that year.
Stamper, Macle, age 7, daughter attended school that year.

We know this census was taken the same year Irene was born and John died.

The family of John and Mary, along with other Stamper and Blevins families lived in Wilkes County, in a place called Basin Creek. It was way down in the mountains but not many miles from the Cranberry, Laurel Springs Area of Alleghany, the top of the mountain is where the Blue Ride Parkway is now. They were living there in 1916 when the area had a great flood and washed the houses away, there were landslides.

The families had to flee for their lives going up the side of the mountain. John and Mary's family, their children and some relatives living with them had to spend the night on the side of the mountain huddled under some trees and bushes with only a few quilts and the clothes on their backs.

In the morning when it was light they climbed the rest of the way out of the mountain, the younger children had to be carried, it was several miles. By the time they reached the top of the mountain the rain had stopped and the sun was shinning brightly.

They went to the home of Aunt Elzina Hoppers, (as told by Macle Stamper Shore, who was one of the small children). If you will remember that Lottie had a daughter Eilzina Hoppers from her first marriage. Listed in the U. S. Census 1880, Alleghany County Cranberry township Elzina Hopper, age eighteen, daughter, living with the Troy Stamper family.

"Aunt Elzina had a large house with porches around three sides and the children slept on the porch". Macle Stamper Shore, said, "Also right out from the house, three counties joined, Alleghany, Wilkes and Ashe. I walked out and tried to stand in all three counties at the same time."

From the things Macle told it appears that many of the families who had lost their houses in the flood, first went to this house. I remember my dad, Onley Stamper, talking about the flood he was about nine years old at the time. He had funny things he remembered about it as well as being frightened. At the time of the flood John's family had a Frankie and Silvester Blevins living with them. Onley told that all night while they were huddled under the bushes on the side of the mountain trying to keep as dry as they could, Silvester, would say over and over, "Frankie, are you all right? Frankie, are you all right?". ".

The family of John and Mary lived in the Whitehead Community of Alleghany County, North Carolina for a while after the flood. We not sure how long they lived there. Macle said they moved from Whitehead to Laurel Springs. Next they moved to a community called Hare.

John had bought a small farm near Hare. At Hare there was a store, mill and a mill pond. The Hare Milling Company was built in 1870 by Calvin Edwards. John did logging, some carpenter work and farming. It has been told that he wore a three piece suit even when he was doing the logging. The family owned some cattle, chickens and pigs. John built a nice two story house, and painted it white. The family was so proud of the house, it was the nicest place they had ever lived.

This house was weatherboard like the houses of their ancestors but it had more rooms. Upstairs there were three rooms, one for the boys, one for the girls and one for which ever relatives were living with them at the time. There was a fireplace for heat, as well as a chimney so they could have a big black cook stove. Mary loved to cook large meals for her family. She was a great cook even the simplest of foods tasted delicious the way she fixed them.

When John built the house he needed some cash for some of the things needed to build with, nails, windows, roofing materials, he had the lumber. Anyway there was a man who lent him the money he needed, it was three hundred dollars. We do not know the name of the man who lent him the money.

John did not live very long after finishing the house. He died of pneumonia, on a cold December day. His sister Laura was living with the family when he died, she had three children, she was divorced. From what his daughter told Mary had gone to the spring to get some water and Laura was at the house with John when he died.

I can know John Ander, from what I have heard of him from his children and from family tradition. Like the Stampers before him he was a short man about five foot seven to eight inches. His hair was dark brown in color which receded early, he had light bright blue eyes which sparked with emotion. I can only imagine he had the same temper as the other Stampers. He took pride in his appearance. His daughters said he most always wore a three piece suit even when he was logging.

He was a loving caring person, caring not only for his wife and children but the other members of his family as well. At the time of his father's death John was caring for him in his home. He had a sense of responsibility when it came to caring for his family. He had family members, Blevins as well as Stampers, living with him most of his married life.

This is a quote from Dr. Clifford Stamper about his father Grover Cleveland Stamper and John Ander Stamper. "My father always talked fondly of John Ander, he was good to him. He said he taught him many things about how to work and about life, he was more like a father then a older brother"[2].

John was a hard worker and he provided for his family well. He was loved and respected by his children. He was a devoted husband. Why the good die young we will never know. John Ander Stamper left his footprints in the soil of his farm at Hare, North Carolina. But most of all he left them in the hearts of his descendants.

John was a Christian, his daughters say he was the best of the Stampers. He did not drink and swear like the rest of them, he was like his mother that way.

Here is a quote from the obituary written by E. E. Wyatt, at the time of John Ander's death.

"Brother J. A. Stamper was born April 3, 1874, died December 12, 1920, making his stay on this earth 46 years, 8 months and 9 days. Married to Mary Blevins February 14, 1897; born unto this union 8 children, 4 boys and 4 girls, all are still living. He made a profession of the Christian religion in 1897, later joining the church at Basin Creek, being baptized; later ordained a deacon, moving his membership to Pleasant Grove, serving faithfully until his death. The Church has lost one of its best members.

Too much could not be said about the good brother; we believe he was a Christian that God had made, and what the Lord has made, He will preserve. We believe what man can make, man can destroy, now he has laid aside his earthly toils, and all his sufferings here below. Brother Stamper was so dear to all who knew him. He left a dear companion, children and a host of friends to mourn his loss. The purpose of this obituary is not for the dead but for the living. Sister Mary we believe you did all you could for him during his sickness, but he has bid you farewell, we believe you will meet again where no more farewell tears are shed, and our loss is his eternal gain. Children I want you to try to gain that peaceful shore where separation will be with papa no more. His body is lying in the Cemetery at Mountain View, the burial service being conducted by Elder A. McKnight and F. M. Osborn."

After John's death, just like the villain in the old movies the man who John owed the money came and took the house from widow Mary and her children. Mary had tried to get the man to take the cattle for the debt as they were worth well over the three hundred owed the villain. When he would not take the cattle for the debt, Mary told him she would sell the cattle and get the money for him. But Oh! No!, he would not hear of it.

He had wanted the nice new house for himself and would not wait for her to sell the cattle. He put Mary and the children out of the house and took the house as well as the land.

Mary sold the cattle and rented a place to live but times were tough for the family. Only a couple weeks after the man moved in to the nice new two story house it burned to the ground, it served him right. (As told by family tradition).

Mary married Daniel Smith after John Ander died. They married about 1922, he was sixteen years older then she was. They did not have any children together. Mary had children ranging in ages from twenty-one years to nine months when John died. The two oldest daughters went to Winston Salem and worked for the R. J. Reynolds Tobacco Company for a while before coming back to Alleghany County and marrying. That left four children still at home. It was very hard for a women at that time to raise children alone.

Mary was a handsome thin women, she had long black hair, which she wore braided or piled up on her head, her complexion was olive, like a permanent suntan. Her big eyes were the bluest blue, the color of the sky on a clear day. Also from family tradition she was part Cherokee Indian from the Blevins side of the family. She played the organ and sang in church. She sang alto in the choir. Mary's daughters told us that she gave singing lessons. It has been told by some of her older granddaughters who can remember her well, that when she was older, she had a pot belly.

According to family tradition, Daniel Smith went to the same church as Mary. He told Mary that if she would marry him, he had some money in the bank and, he would take care of her and the children. After they were married Mary found out that Daniel got his money by bootlegging moonshine whiskey. This made for much unhappiness since Mary did not believe in anyone drinking whiskey. I believe otherwise they were good companions, and had a comfortable live life together.

Daniel's first wife, Alice had died in 1920 the same year as John. His children were older then Mary's, his grandchildren sometimes played with Mary's younger children.

Mary, Daniel and the children moved several times from Hare to Saddle Mountain and different houses in the area. I am not sure if they ever owned a house during those years while they were moving around.

Onley said his mother was a very good cook, but he did not like fancy cooking. What he remembered liking best was the corn bread which was left on the back of the cook stove, after supper. The next morning when his mother made the gravy he would put it on the leftover corn bread.

After the children were grown, Mary's youngest son, Bacle built a house for Mary and Daniel. Bacle was only eighteen years old when he built that house. It was really a nice little house with a front and back porch. There were three rooms downstairs and two upstairs.

Daniel did not live many years after the house was built. He died in 1936 at the age of 77. When he died, Mary had him buried beside his first wife Alice, the mother of his children. They are buried in the cemetery of Saddle Mountain Church just off the Blue Ridge Parkway, in Alleghany County.

After Daniel died Mary did not like living alone. She was not afraid to live alone, it was that it was so lonely living alone. She lived for short periods with different ones of her sons in Maryland.

Our family was living in Maryland at the time I was four or five years old. Mary, my grandmother was living with my Uncle Bacle Stamper at the time. I can remember visiting them. I also remember my grandmother visiting us one Sunday, she and my dad went fishing and they took me along. I was happy that they had taken me fishing. What I remember most about that day is talking with my grandmother and wanting her to like me. When we got home from fishing she told my mother that I had acted like a little lady, so that made my day. I never spent much time with my grandmother Smith, as I called her. She was a pretty women and everyone only had nice things to say about her.

She moved back to her house the one her son Bacle had built for her. She had a women living with her there so she would not have to live alone. I can remember visiting her there also. I remember going to one Sunday dinner in the summer time and her setting a table on the front porch, it was loaded down with food. There were uncle, aunts and cousins there also. She was diabetic and took insulin. I remember that she boiled the needles and syringes, no disposable ones in those days.

She died of a stroke on 18 November 1941, she had a stroke about a week earlier and then she had a second stoke which she died from. I can remember her funeral well it was the first funeral I had ever been to. It was a rainy day, it was like the whole world was crying because she had died.

Quote from Shirley Stamper Harris one of Mary's granddaughters. "Some of the first things I remember are visiting my grandmother when she had her stroke. My mother held me up so I could see her and she rubbed my face with her unaffected hand. And then in a few days going to her funeral.[11]" John and Mary are buried side by side in Mountain View church cemetery near Roaring Gap, North Carolina.

JOHN (ANDER) ANDREW STAMPER AS A YOUNG MAN

THE FAMILY OF JOHN (ANDER) ANDREW STAMPER

From left to right: **John Ander with Inize on his lap, Lynn, Mary with Onley on her lap, Mother's helper (we do not have her name) she has Virdie on her lap, Bert is in front of Mary.**

(taken 1907)

LAURA[8] STAMPER, (Troy[7]), (Hiram H.[6]), (John[5]), (Jonathan Jr.[4]), (Jonathan Sr.[3]), (Powell[2]), (John[1]) the daughter of Troy and Lottie was born 16 September 1872 and died 20 February 1958. She married Fielden Caudill, they were later divorced.

Laura and Fielden had three children; (1) Bert Caudill was born about 1900, he is still living at the time of this writing. He married and lived near Edgewood, Maryland he had several children. That is all the information I have about his family. (2) Fred Caudill born 9 October 1905, died 4 July 1961, he never married. What we know of Fred is, he was just a drunk and did not do anything useful with his life. He is buried beside his mother at Mountain View cemetery near Roaring Gap, North Carolina. (3) Fronia Caudill born about 1907, she married Clay Joines, no other information.

Laura lived with her brother John's family at times before he died. Macle Stamper Shore said her mother would have her spend the night with Aunt Laura's family when she was a child, and she did not like to do that. She said that Aunt Laura did not like to cook and that they might only have biscuits to eat. Laura did have a little house of her own at various times. My parents spent their honeymoon at a cabin that belonged to her. I can remember, as a child, visiting her when she lived at Rich Hill, North Carolina. She had a little two room cabin made of unpainted weatherboards.

After Aunt Laura was an old lady she stayed with different ones of John's children. All John's children knew Aunt Laura. We do not know why she did not live with her children. She is buried beside her son Fred and near two of her brothers at Mountain View Cemetery near Roaring Gap, North Carolina.

HARRY (MONROE)[8] STAMPER, (Troy[7]), (Hiram H.[6]), (John[5]), (Jonathan Jr.[4]), (Jonathan Sr.[3]), (Powell[2]), (John[1]) was the son of Troy and Charlotte (Lottie) Wagoner Hoppers Stamper. We have not found Monroe living with Troy's family in any of the census. The only information we have on him is from family tradition, and his tombstone. He was born in 1867 and died December 7, 1947 of a stroke. He is buried in Mountain View Cemetery near Roaring Gap, North Carolina, beside his brother John A. and sister Laura. It was his request to be brought back to the mountains of North Carolina to be buried.

He married three times: first to Canna Conley, divorced, she was the mother of his three daughters. Monroe and Canna's children were; (1) Pearl, no birth or death dates, she married a Sprat and had three sons and one daughter; (2) Jessie, no birth or death dates, she married a Ryan and had three daughters; (3) Lettie, no death dates, she married a Lambert and had two sons and one daughter[13].

Second he married Elizabeth (Kattie) Katharine Clyburn. After her death he was single for many years. Ten months before he died he married a lovely nurse, Amanda Mullens, from Hinton, West Virginia, who was much younger than he was. After they were married they moved to Galax, Virginia, and lived there until Monroe died. Amanda worked in the hospital in Galax [13].

Monroe and Canna were living together with their three daughters in West Virginia. Monroe was doing carpenter work and Canna was keeping house and caring for the girls. Pearl was a big girl about seven or eight years old and Lettie was a baby in the playpen on the porch. Monroe saddled his horse and said to Jessie, (who was about five years old), "Would you like to go for a ride with Daddy?" Monroe set Jessie on the horse in front of him and Pearl watched them ride off. That is the last Pearl saw of them until many years later when she was a grown woman[13].

The next day Canna left the other two girls with friends and she went in search of Monroe and Jessie. She was gone for three days and when she came home she told Pearl that her daddy and little sister were dead and for her to never speak of them again.

Monroe took Jessie and he married Elizabeth Katharine (Kattie). Kattie raised Jessie as if she were her own daughter. Monroe and Kattie had no children together. Kattie was the love of Monroe's life, they had many happy years together. Kattie lived to see Jessie have three daughters. Jessie's family lived near Monroe and Kattie and they had a close relationship with their granddaughters[13].

This information is from Monroe's granddaughter, Helen Meadows, in Shady Springs. West Virginia: Monroe moved to West Virginia about 1891 or 1892. A quote from his granddaughter "He did mention a sister Laura and said that he left North Carolina to keep from killing her husband. He must have had a serious reason because I never knew a less violent man. I do remember my grandfather said he had a grandmother who could not speak English, that must have been the Dutch lady. He was a very skilled carpenter and that is the only kind of work he ever did".

Copied from the U. S. Census at the National Archives in Washington D.C. 1920 Census for West Virginia, county; Raleigh, city; Beckley. Vol. 47, E D 163, Sheet 11, Line 64: Stamper, Harry Monroe, white male, age 48, born North Carolina Stamper, Elizabeth Kattie, white female, age 40, born West Virginia

Macle Stamper Shore said she went and spent one year with her Uncle Monroe is West Virginia when she was about eleven years old. Monroe was married to Kattie at that time. This must have been about the time Macle's mother, Mary, married Daniel Smith.

I can remember Monroe visiting us one time in North Carolina. I was a child at the time. I am not sure of the year it was some time in the early nineteen forties. Monroe was my father's uncle.

GROVER CLEVELAND (CLEVE)^{8} STAMPER, (Troy^{7}) (Hiram H.^{6}) (John^{5}) (Jonathan Jr.^{4}), (Jonathan Sr.^{3}), (Powell^{2}), (John^{1}), the son of Troy and Median Pruitt Stamper was born 7 September 1890 and died 1 June 1961. He married Bessie Ashley. Cleve's father Troy died when he was nine years old. Cleve lived with his older half brother John Ander's family for four or five years. After that Cleve's mother answered an advertisement in a paper from a man, Mr. Ashley, who wanted someone to live with him to help with work around the house and to care for his invalid wife. They would receive room, board and a small amount of cash. His mother took the job, which was in Ashe County. Cleve went to Ashe County with his mother and lived out the rest of his life in Ashe County[2].

The information we have on the family of Grover Cleveland Stamper as well as much other information about the Stampers came from Dr. Clifford Stamper. He is Cleve's son. He is a dentist living and practicing in Morganton, North Carolina.

Cleve and Bessie Ashley Stamper had twelve children, at this time we do not have all the birth dates and are not sure of order of birth: (1) Edward Earl born 1924, died 1962, he married Margaret Sisk. (2) Shirley born 1940, died at age 30, she married Bennie Barker. (3) John William lives in Austin, Texas. (4) Bryan is deceased, he lived in Lansing, North Carolina. (5) James Monroe lives in Edgewood, Maryland. (6) Dr. Robert L. lived in Ashe County, North Carolina. and Atlanta, Georgia. (7) Dr. Clifford is a dentist, he lives in Morganton, North Carolina. (8) Ann married Earl King and lives in Lansing, North Carolina. (9) Viola married Robert Lawson and lives in Corpus Christie, Texas. (10) Rose married George Schisler and lives in Atlanta, Georgia. (11) Janeavee (Jan) married Paul Brooks and lives in Wilkesboro, North Carolina. (12) Frances married an Edwards and lives in Warrensville, North Carolina.

A quote from Macle Stamper Shore, "Uncle Cleve married an Ashley, I think she was a teacher they had twelve children and they all went to college".

Cleve's daughter Rose said that her father was a school teacher and her mother was a housewife caring for the home and a large family.

Dr. Robert L. Stamper, the son of Cleve and Bessie Stamper, the brother of Dr. Clifford Stamper, is a minister in Presbyterian Church and is well known for his many community services. He is a former vice-president of Columbia Theological Seminary, a former vice-president of the Kings College and a formed president of Bible Seminary in New York City. He has also helped to turn four inactive churches into community centers at Apple Grove, Husk, White Top, Virginia and Lansing, Virginia[10].

LILA[8] STAMPER, (John Baxter[7]) (Hiram T.[6]) (William[5])(Jonathan Jr.[4]) (Jonathan Sr.[3]) (Powell[2]), (John[1]) the oldest child of John Baxter and Martha Ann Jordan Stamper. She was born 27 April 1904 in Georgia. As of January 1993, she is still living, in Ball Grand, Georgia. She married Paul Grogan, who was born 4 May 1902 and died 20 March 1956[12]. Lila and Paul had two sons; (1) Hiram John Grogan born 21 August 1925, he is a retired Psychologist and attorney with Georgia State Probations Department. He married Ruth Carney, she is a retired teacher. (2) Lee Roy Grogan born April 1931, he married Jane Haywood. They have a daughter who is a nurse and a son who is in hospital administration[12].

LOUELLA[8] RICHARDSON, (Nancy (Nalie)[7] Choate), (Margaret (Peggy)[6]Fender), (Martha[5]Toliver), (Frances (Frankie)[4] **STAMPER**), (Jonathan Sr.[3]), (Powell[2]), (John[1]) was the sixth child of Henry R. Richardson and Nancy (Nalia) Choate Richardson. She was the great-great-great granddaughter of Jonathan Stamper Sr. She was born 2 October 1881 and died 2 March 1960. She married Robert L. Hanks 25 September 1898. His parents were Dr. Hugh Hanks and Martha Jane Sturgill Hanks. He was born 2 October 1876 and died 14 August 1966.

Robert and Louella Richardson Hanks had four children, all born in Alleghany County. (1) Ima V. born 29 October 1900. She married Roscoe Lee Smith 21 January 1916. (2) Earn Hanks born 13 May 1904 died 10 February 1976. He married Maye Miles, she was the sister of Paul and Raymond Miles. Paul and Raymond married Stamper sisters Virdie and Inize, the daughters of John Ander. (3) Arthur Hanks born 31 January 1908. He married Ruth McKnight. (4) Eva (Faye) Hanks born 20 February 1912. She died in 1993. She married Major A. Blevins in 1929, the son of Quincy and Emma Combs Blevins. Mary Blevins who married John Ander Stamper was Quincy's aunt.

ABRAHAM[8] STAMPER, (Masterson (Bad Mat)[7]), (Jean (Jennie[6]), (Joshua[5]), (Jonathan Jr.[4]), (Jonathan Sr.[3]), (Powell[2]), (John[1]) was the son of Masterson (Bad Mat) Stamper and Jane Rutherford Stamper. Abraham was born about 1870. He married Ruth (Emaline) Dolinger, lived in Grayson County, Virginia. They had at least one son named William Harrison he was born 25 May 1889 and died 1 September 1937. After Emaline's death Abraham married Cora Baugas, they were both older when they married and did not have any children.

ABRAHAM AND HIS SECOND WIFE CORA BAUGAS STAMPER

ONLEY EUGENE STAMPER
as a young man (taken before 1934)

ONLEY EUGENE AND ELIZABETH SHAW STAMPER
(taken November 1963)

CHAPTER 9

NINTH GENERATION

ONLEY EUGENE^{9} STAMPER, (John (Ander) Andrew^{8}), (Troy^{7}), (Hiram H.^{6}), (John^{5}), (Jonathan Jr.^{4}), (Jonathan Sr.^{3}), (Powell^{2}), (John^{1}) the fifth child of John Ander and Mary Emiline Blevins Stamper born 12 September 1907, died 9 February 1964. His nickname was Gabe, this is what his friends called him. He married Elizabeth (Liza) Etta Shaw, the daughter of John Alexander Shaw and Martha Fender Shaw. Onley and Elizabeth were married 30 March 1934, in Alleghany County, North Carolina. Their witnesses were Onley's sister Inize Stamper Miles and her husband Raymond Miles. They were married by Glenn Nickols J. P. at the Court House, Sparta, North Carolina.

Elizabeth was working for Onley's sister Virdie, at the time of their marriage as a mother's helper. She was working for a dollar a week, plus her room and board. She said that she worked for ten weeks to pay for her wedding dress, which was blue silk. It was the depression, and at the time ten dollars was a lot of money. Onley was working at Roaring Gap golf course for a dollar a day. They went on a honeymoon for a week, to a cabin that belonged to Onley's Aunt Laura Stamper Caudill. The cabin was located at a place called Sweet Hallow, it was some place near Laurel Springs, North Carolina.

Onley and Elizabeth had two daughters: (1) Betty Sue born 21 March 1935, in Alleghany County at Cherry Lane, North Carolina. Betty married George Henry Latham, 10 July 1951.
(2) Shirley Jean born 25 June 1938, in Hartford County at Churchville, Maryland. Shirley married Olen Vaughn Harris, 28 September 1956.

Onley was twenty six years old when he married. He had traveled across the United Stated and back, before he meet Elizabeth, she was nineteen. I believe he would say he had bummed around for several years. He left home when he was sixteen. He had lied about his age and gotten into the Army. He really hated the Army and did not try to adjust to it. He wrote and asked his mother to see what she could do to get him out. We do not know how but she was able to get him out. I believe he spent less then six weeks in the Army. After this he worked in Winston-Salem for the R. J. Reynolds Tobacco Company for a while. He chewed tobacco, perhaps that is when he stared. He may have smoked first, before changing to chewing tobacco. He said he liked living in Winston-Salem and had a good time after work going to the movies. Western movies were his favorites.

He once went to see a live western show with Tom Mix and his Wonder Horse. Many years later he told his children about this show and about all the tricks the horse could do.

Why he quit working in the factory and moved on I don't know. One could surmise that it was that Stamper thing about being restless and looking for adventure. Or was it wanting to see new places or maybe find a better job?

Another thing he told about was living in Baltimore, Maryland and being a companion to a wealthy old women. She bought him attractive clothes and took him out to meticulous places. He said that she wanted him to stay with her but he got bored with it, and moved on.

He hitchhiked and hoboed across the United States. He told of how he would ride in the boxcars, ride on top of the trains or ride the blinds. There were other men doing the same thing. If these men were caught they would be thrown off the train. Those were the depression years. Times were hard and there were times when a job could not be found. Onley told how he would be in a strange town and nervelessly go up to the door of one of the nicer looking houses and knock on the door hoping a woman would answer the door. A woman might give him a handout sooner then a man would. The hoboes had some sort of signal as to which houses would give a handout, so he would try these houses first. He wanted to do some sort of work for a meal. In winter there might be some wood that he could chop. In summer a garden to be hoed or grass to be cut. The food that was given to him would be simple food, beans, potatoes, bread etc. and some coffee in an old tin cup. If he was very lucky a farmer would allow him to sleep in the barn. If it was planting or harvest time he might stay on and help the farmer for a week or two.

There were several years that Onley's mother did not even hear from him. But there would come a day when he would send some money home. If he did pick up a part time job and made a little money, he sent some to his mother. His two younger sisters tell of him coming home once with a car and they were so proud and excited. Irene, his youngest sister said he brought her a bride doll when he came home one time. It was the only store bought doll she had ever had. She said she kept it for many years, until it rotted. From the above we can see that Onley cared about his family.

Onley rarely got upset with Elizabeth, she was the love of his life. He let her have her way in most things and did spoil her. She did not ask for many material things. So when she wanted something Onley could not get he was sad, because of it.

Onley had a very quick temper and would fly in a rage when something or someone upset him. Everyone was thankful that the anger was over as quickly as it started. His temper got him into trouble a few times as a young man. With age his temper dampened and he was easier to get along with.

Soon after their marriage Onley left Elizabeth and went to Maryland to look for a better paying job. He was able to get a job milking cows at a dairy farm owned by Sam Fielder. He would get a house with electric lights and wood for heat and all the milk the family needed and forty dollars a month. This was better then he was able to do in North Carolina. At that time electric lights were something only the people who lived in town had in North Carolina.

Elizabeth joined Onley within a month. She told of the trip to Maryland. She had never been over seventy five miles away from where she was born before. She said there was a bus that went from Sparta, North Carolina to Belair, Maryland. It was like a van which could carry six people. She told how she, one other women and three men and the bus driver made the trip. They had to stop and spend one night on the way. The place they stayed was like a motel, called cabins she and the other women shared a room. This was an adventure for Elizabeth and she was happy when she got to Maryland to be with Onley.

Onley worked very long hours on the farm, he was up by four in the morning to go milk. His working days were twelve hours long, some times even longer, seven days a week. Elizabeth was alone all that time and she was lonely. So when she got pregnant she wanted to go back to North Carolina to have the baby.

So they moved back to Cherry Lane, North Carolina so that Elizabeth would be near someone she knew when she had her first child. The little old house where Elizabeth had her first child, Betty Sue, is still standing in Cherry Lane. Fifty five years later Betty's daughter lived in that same little house for about one year.

From this time on Onley and Elizabeth moved back and forth to Maryland and Onley worked at many different jobs. He mostly did labor type work, for he had very little education. He was a fair carpenter, and worked with his brother Bacle building houses, sometimes.

When their second and last child, Shirley Jean, was born they were living in Maryland. Onley was working on a farm again milking cows. Onley had gone to North Carolina and brought Elizabeth's mother (Martha Fender Shaw) back to Maryland to be with her when the baby was born.

Elizabeth had to go to the hospital in Baltimore and spend some time before the baby was born. Elizabeth's mother, Martha was there to look after their daughter Betty.

The baby was born at home, Dr. Hudson delivered the baby. A very beautiful girl with black curly hair, and the bluest eyes, the color of the sky on a clear day. They named her Shirley Jean, Jean for Onley Eugene. By the time she was a few months old the black hair had turned blond. Elizabeth's health was not good and the doctor had told her that her heart could not stand her being pregnant another time. This is why they did not have any more children after Shirley .

Mostly Elizabeth was a housewife and worked hard around the house, gardening, keeping the lawn mowed etc. There were a few times she worked outside the home when they lived in Maryland. She worked in a shoe factory for a short time. She also worked as a waitress at various times. She did baby sitting many different times.

Onley could read and write just enough to get by. He had gone to school very little, after his father died. Elizabeth loved to read, since Onley did not enjoy reading he could not see why anyone else did. One of the happiest times of my childhood was when my mother read to me.

When the family was living in North Carolina there were ways to make a little money, so Elizabeth could give her girls some spending money and little extras. There is an evergreen leaf that grows on a long steam on the ground called Galax. They are used in floral arrangements. There were some places that bought Galax leaves all year around. The leaves had to be pulled up from the ground by wrapping a finger around the steam and pulling it straight up. It was a back breaking job, and the steams would cut in to the fingers until they bleed. They were sold by the thousand and if someone was fast at it, there was good money to be made. After the supper dishes were washed, the sack of leaves would be poured out in the floor. Everyone in the family would set in the floor and pack the leaves in to twenty five leaves per pack. The pack of leaves was tied with a string which had been saved when the cow feed was opened. The packs of leaves were then packed again into a box or basket so they would be easy to take to the store. Elizabeth would often give the money from the Galax to the girls for school clothes, school supplies, and a little spending money. Betty and Shirley learned to pull Galax at an early age, and often pulled them in the fall to get extra money for school things.

The family had a few chickens and there were more eggs than they could eat. Elizabeth would give the eggs to the girls to take to the store to sale. They were allowed to use the money for things they needed.

There were many different herbs, plants and barks that could be gathered to sell. One was shanahaw it is a bush like plant which grows to the size of a small tree. The shanahaw had to be dug up by the roots. The bark of the tops, and the roots, were both sold. The bush was dug up by the roots and the top was cut from the roots with an ax. The tops were cut in to pieces easy to handle then the bark was pealed off with a knife. The bark from the roots was beaten off with a hammer.

In winter when Onley was out of work he would dig the shanahaw. In the evening when it was too cold to get the bark off the sticks outside it would be brought inside and again all the family worked on getting the bark off the sticks and roots. They would set on the floor around the potbellied wood stove, by the light of coal oil lamps and peel or beat off the bark.

In the fall of the year many places bought pine tips (the ends of the pine branches) to be made into pine garlands for the upcoming Christmas season. Also they would buy pine cones by the bushel. This was a way to make a little extra money for Christmas gifts.

Another thing Onley would do in winter was hunt. The meat from most animals was eaten to supplement the diet of dried beans, potatoes, canned vegetables which had come from the garden, corn bead and milk. The hides were stretched on boards and sold for their fur.

Often Elizabeth would make the girls dresses from printed cow and chicken feed sacks. The dresses turned out looking really nice. The girls were always pleased with the new dresses even if they were made of feed sacks.

Onley and Elizabeth were good Christen parents who took their daughters to church and Sunday school on Sunday morning. They attended Mount Carmel Missionary Baptist Church near Roaring Gap, North Carolina.

The family, and doing things together, was what life was all about for Onley and Elizabeth. Onley loved Christmas time and playing Santa Clause. He and the girls would go out in the fields and hunt a Christmas tree each year. The family had fun decorating the tree.

The first year in North Carolina that they had electric so they could have lights on the tree, was the Christmas of 1947. That was an exciting time Onley even got some outside lights so they put lights on two little trees beside the fount porch. He always made the fudge on Christmas Eve and the next morning there would be two pieces of fudge missing. Onley would tell the girls that Santa had helped himself to the fudge. There was not a lot money for Christmas gifts but Santa always left something for the girls. Another happy time for the family was going on picnics in the summer.

One of the things Onley liked best of all was fish. He had always like to fish from the time he was a young boy. His sister Macle tells of the times she went fishing with him. One time she remembers well, is the time she fell in the creek and Onley was so angry with her for frightening the trout, he made her return to the house.

The winter of 1957 after their youngest daughter had married, Onley and Elizabeth went to Florida for the winter. Onley had said for years, "When the girls are grown, we will go to Florida for the winter". Two of Onley's brothers, two or three nephews and some nieces went along at the same time.

The Stampers made a caravan, and went to Florida. They all had a good time. Several of them say that winter was one of the happiest times of their lives. Vird, one of Onley's sisters, joined them and spent a few weeks down there also.

The thing that everyone enjoyed most was fishing. When they went deep sea fishing Onley got seasick. He blamed it on the tobacco he was chewing, and he never chewed tobacco again. Elizabeth was happy that he stopped chewing tobacco, she never liked the fact that he chewed the stuff. Can you imagine what it would be like to kiss some one who chewed tobacco? It gives me much delight to know that they got to make that trip and it was such a happy time for them.

The years after this went by rapidly for them. They bought a different house and worked on fixing it up. Onley worked for his brother Bacle doing carpenter work. Elizabeth worked around the house. She did gardening and she planted lots of flowers. What she enjoyed most was baby-sitting her grandsons John and Mark. They were her daughter Shirley's sons. When Onley did not work he enjoyed helping care for the boys. He had missed not having a son, and having the grandsons made up for that. He would take John out to help him work in the yard and build fences. John said, the time he spent with his grandfather are pleasant memories for him.

Elizabeth was never very healthy, she was diabetic, had heart trouble and high blood pressure. Onley was fairly healthy but he had pneumonia frequently. One time he fell off the roof of a house he was working on, and broke some ribs. He took pneumonia after that and was very sick. Elizabeth was afraid he would die but he recovered. In 1962 he broke his leg, and was out of work for several months. He also recovered from that. When his leg healed he went back to work for his brother.

On an unusually warm spring like day, Sunday 9 February 1964, Onley and his son-in-law, Olen Harris, went fishing. They went away down in the mountains where there would be lots of mountain trout. They had planned the fishing trip the day before.

Elizabeth went to spend the day with Shirley and the boys. It was a little after noon when they came to tell Elizabeth that Onley had a heart attack and died while he was fishing. He died doing the thing he enjoyed doing best. He was only fifty-six years old, a man taken from his family in his prime. This was a terrible shock for the family. It was almost more then Elizabeth could bare but she did get through it. The rest of her life was lonely for the only man she ever loved.

Onley had been a good neighbor he was always willing to offer a hand when the neighbors needed help. When anyone in the neighborhood died he would go help dig the grave. He was a loving husband, and help mate to Elizabeth. He was a good father, giving his children love and some little extras in life. One thing I think my sister, Shirley would be glad for me to add here, is on her birthday 25 June he would buy her all the ice cream she could eat. The rest of the family had ice cream that day too but it was Shirley's special day. I have tried to be objective in telling what I know of Onley's life. It is not as easy to be objective when it is my father I am writing about. He left his footprints in Alleghany County and the many places he traveled in his youth.

Onley never made a lot of money, but he and Elizabeth were good managers. They owned five different homes and several house trailers during their life together. When Onley died he left no debts, their home was paid for and he owned other land where he had planned to build a new house.

Elizabeth wanted to keep the house she had lived in with Onley but she was very much afraid to live alone. The first year after Onley died her daughter Shirley and family moved in with her. Shirley wanted her own house and after a year they moved out. After that Elizabeth spent time at Shirley's house or one of the grandchildren would spend the night with her. Her days were filled with caring for her grandsons while Shirley worked.

In the fall of 1967 Elizabeth's other daughter Betty and her family built a house next door to her. Now she had other grandchildren near to look after. She gave a lot of love and caring to the grandchildren and they gave her a purpose in life. Since the houses were side by side Elizabeth would spend the day at her house and fix it up and do the things she liked to do. Then in the evening when it was time for Betty's children to come home from school she would go over to their house. This allowed Betty to work and not have to worry about the children.

So things worked out well for everyone. The next twenty years went by without many crisis. Elizabeth was sick a lot but she had more good times then bad.

Elizabeth and all her grandchildren were able to have a close relationship. Even after the grandchildren were all grown and no longer at home she still spent the nights at Betty's house and the days at hers.

Elizabeth's daughters tried to make her life as pleasant for her as they could. They took her on trips and spent time with her. What gave Elizabeth the most pleasure was spending time with her grandchildren. She often said if it had not been for the grandchildren she would not have made it, they gave her reason to live.

Elizabeth often spent her weekends with Shirley. If she did not spend her weekend with Shirley, Shirley would go spend Sunday afternoon with her. Shirley would do things around the house for her like wash windows, paint or paper the walls.

Elizabeth was honored on 25 November 1981 at Mount Caramel Baptist Church for being a member for fifty years. Her picture was in the newspaper.

George, Betty's husband was out of work in North Carolina. He was laid off from his job for several months and in danger of losing everything they had if he did not find a job. He had a job offer in Southern Maryland. He took the job in Maryland and he and Betty moved there. Their move was very traumatic for Elizabeth. She cried tears of despair, saying she could not live alone. She said she would sell everything she had and give it to the girls. They all agreed that she would spend six months of the year with each daughter. So history repeats itself, she moved to Maryland with Betty and George.

On 20 September 1986 Elizabeth moved to Maryland. Betty and Elizabeth were able to have some quality time together and were very close. Elizabeth seemed happy. She often said, "Who would believe I would end up back in Maryland after all these years". It was at this time that she told Betty what it was like for her when she first moved to Maryland after her marriage.

Thanksgiving that year they went back to North Carolina for a visit. Their plans were for Elizabeth to live with Betty until Easter of 1987, and then go stay with Shirley until September.

After Thanksgiving, they had been back to Maryland about a week when Elizabeth had a heart attack. Her doctor sent her to George Washington University Hospital in Washington, D. C. There she underwent coronary artery bypass surgery, 12 December 1986. Shirley flew up to be with her for a few days. Elizabeth was released from the hospital the next week. She seemed to recover from the surgery but the doctor could not seem to get her medication adjusted so she felt well.

Betty was working in a small hospital at the time and did not want to quit her job. Her daughter Georgia came to stay and help out while Elizabeth was recovering from the surgery. Georgia and Elizabeth dropped Betty off at the hospital to go to work. Then Georgia took Elizabeth for her doctor's appointment.

Elizabeth was with the doctor, it was while the doctor was checking her over, she had another heart attack. She went in to congestive heart failure. They rushed her to the hospital which was less then a block away.

Everything that could be done was done, never the less, about 7 P. M., 9 February 1987 she died. Her body was taken to North Carolina so she could be buried beside Onley. She had died on the anniversary of his death. He had died twenty three years earlier. They are buried in the cemetery at Mount Caramel Baptist Church, near Roaring Gap, North Carolina.

Quote from Shirley Stamper Harris, "Mother was always quoting the Bible. She and I spent many hours talking about death and heaven. Mother was a great teacher, and may I always remember the things she taught me about live and about faith in life eternal[11]".

One of the most important things she taught me, which has stayed with me to this day, is the Golden Rule. I believe that I am a better person for trying to follow it.

This is the eulogy written for Elizabeth by her only granddaughter Georgia Sue Latham, MD.

Elizabeth Shaw Stamper

Humming birds in her flower garden,
Church on Sunday mornings,
Family picnics on the Parkway,
She enjoyed the simple pleasures of life.
She enjoyed working hard,
And doing things for others,
Always wanting to give more,
Than she received.

She loved her daughters, Betty and Shirley,
Her grandchildren:
Tom, Gene, Georgia, John, Mark, David and Sandy,
and her great grandchildren:
Lori, Tina, Candida, and Garrett.
She cared for all of us as babies,
And taught us lessons of life.
We admired her independence, strength of character,
And her sense of fairness.

Although always surrounded by her family and friends,
Her life was lonely after she lost her beloved husband.
With whom she'd shared the joys and struggles of life
for nearly thirty years.
And exactly twenty three years, later she was finely
rejoined with the man she loved so dearly.

We're thankful for the years she was here with us,
And thankful now that she will never suffer or be lonely again.
She will be missed greatly,
But she will live on in each of us.

Excerpt from the will of Elizabeth Stamper written 29 October 1981.

All residue of the property which I may own at the time of my death, real or personal, tangible and intangible, of whatsoever nature and wheresoever situated, to be sold in such a manner as my Executrix feels is in the best interest of my estate and the proceeds be divided between my daughters, Betty Latham and Shirley Harris.

Shirley Harris	Executrix	Written 29 October 1981
Glenda Fenny	Witness	Signed same day
Donald Miles	Witness	
R. B. Duncan	Witness	Elizabeth Stamper

LINVILLE KEMP (LYNN)[9] STAMPER, (John (Ander) Andrew [8]), (Troy[7]), (Hiram H.[6]), (John[5]), (Jonathan Jr.[4]), (Jonathan Sr.[3]), (Powell[2]), (John[1]) was the oldest child of John Ander (Andrew) Stamper and Mary Emiline Blevins Stamper. He was born 27 November 1897 in Alleghany County, North Carolina. He married Effie Lutricia Hendrix, born 6 May 1905, died in Baptist Hospital Winston Salem, North Carolina 4 February 1970. She was the daughter of Edward (Ed) Hendrix and

Matronia (May) Rector Hendrix.

Lynn and Effie had four children: (1) Velma Mae died as infant, buried Macedonia, Iowa. (2) Ina Grace, born 4 May 1925, in Iowa. She married Earnest Brackins, 12 September 1942, they had four children. She died of a brain tumor in Baptist Hospital Winston-Salem, North Carolina 13 September 1974. (3) Virginia, born 27 August 1927 in Iowa. She married Hugh Perry and they had seven children, two died as infants. She and Hugh divorced, she then married Frank Hendrix, they had no children. (4) John Edward born 24 March 1930 in Iowa. He married Cora Mae Ramey she was born 12 May 1933, they married 7 October 1951. John and Cora Mae had four children.

Lynn Stamper was a sergeant in the U. S. Army during World War I. He joined the service when he was about sixteen, his father was still living when he joined. Lynn was also in the Navy. He received a disability pension of some sort because of injuries received while serving in the Military service.

Family members say that Lynn's mother, Mary made all the children bow down beside their beds each night and pray for Lynn and his brother Bert's safe return from the military service.

A quote from Lynn as told to his son John and John's wife Cora Mae, "I was in the Army in 1918, in Boston, Massachusetts. President Woodrow Wilson returned from a trip to France to Boston and I was selected to be one of the Army guards for him while he was there. The secret service men were the only ones that were allowed on the fourth and fifth floors of the building he stayed in. I got to see the President up close and I'll never forget what a long face he had."

The reason I (this writer) always believed in mermaids is Uncle Lynn told stories of seeing them when he was at sea during the war (World War I). He was a very religious man and I could not imagine him telling stories that were not true. He was fun loving and full of life. He loved to tell stories of when he was young and when he was at sea in the Navy.

Lynn's brother Bert Stamper married Effie's sister Carrie Ann Hendrix. Soon after they were married the Ed Hendrix family moved to Iowa. Lynn, Effie, Bert, and Carrie also moved with them. Rance Hendrix who was Ed's Hendrix's brother took the whole family by wagon to Galax, Virginia, (about twenty miles) so they could catch a train to Iowa.

After they arrived in Iowa the Hendrix family bought a farm and raised large fields of corn. Lynn worked some on the farm and he did other things too, like sell vacuum cleaners. He did carpenter work as many of the Stampers before had done and some would do in the future. All Lynn and Effie's children were born in Iowa. Their second daughter Virginia, said they lived there until she was in the third grade of school.

Onley Stamper, Lynn's younger brother said he visited Lynn's family while he was doing his traveling around the country. He said he stayed most of the winter and talked of how cold it was there. Onley said Lynn set around and read a lot that winter, as it was too cold to work outside. The wind blew the snow over the fields were the corn had been cut earlier in the fall. From family tradition, that winter, Lynn, Bert and Onley made a still, so they could make some moonshine whisky from some of the corn.

Lynn knew a lot about his ancestors. He had the names of his grandfathers going back to Powell Stamper. He had bought and put up the grave stone for his grandfather Troy Stamper. He visited and cleaned off the old Stamper graves.

Effie died seventeen years before Lynn, though he was lonely for her, he was an independent old man. He lived alone as long as he was able to care for himself.

Lynn had two different houses, one in the mountains of Alleghany County near the Virginia line where he liked to stay in the summer. He had another below the mountain in Surry County at State Road, North Carolina where he lived in the winter . Every summer he planted a garden, so he could have fresh vegetables. He did his own cooking and housework. After he was no longer able to drive a car, he lived in an apartment in Sparta, North Carolina.

When his health no longer permitted him to live alone he lived in Meadow Brook Nursing home, in Sparta, North Carolina. He died in Alleghany County Memorial Hospital 25 June 1987. He is buried in the same cemetery as his parents, his wife Effie, and Effie's parents, at Mountain View Primitive Church Cemetery, near Roaring Gap, North Carolina.

STAMPER BROTHERS AND SISTERS, FATHER JOHN ANDER
LINVILLE, BACLE, IRENE AND MACLE
(taken 24 July 1985)

SCHLEY (BERT) AND CARRIE HENDREX STAMPER
(taken on their wedding day)

SCHLEY (BERT) BERTIE[9] STAMPER, (John (Ander) Andrew [8]), (Troy[7]), (Hiram H.[6]), (John[5]), (Jonathan Jr.[4]), (Jonathan Sr.[3]), (Powell[2]), (John[1]) the second child of John Ander and Mary Emiline Blevins Stamper. He was born about 1900 and died in 1958, of cancer. He is buried at Belair, Maryland. He married Carrie Ann Hendrix on 15 September 1929. She was the daughter of Edward (Edd) Hendrix and Matronia (Mae) Rector Hendrix. Carrie was the sister of Effie Hendrix who married Bert's brother Lynn.

Carrie's parents Edward (Edd) Hendrix and Matronia (Mae) Rector Hendrix, were married in Alleghany, North Carolina, 21 September 1904. Edd Hendrix was born 1879 and died 1962. Mae Rector was born 1886 and died 1969. They are buried in Mountain View Cemetery, near Roaring Gap, North Carolina. They had nine children:(1) Claudia, a male, born on 4 March 1904 he was about six months old when he died; (2) Effie Lutricia; (3) Viola; (4) Carrie Ann; (5) Edna; (6) Fay; (7) Seymour; (8) Ray; (9) Grace.

When Bert was not much more then a boy near the end of World War I, he joined the Army with his brother Lynn. It has been passed down that they were on a ship going overseas when the war was over and the ship turned around and came back.

Bert and Carrie had five children: (1) Lonzo, born 1 April 1930 in Carson Iowa. He married two times, first Elsie Gentry and had three sons. Next he married Maude Scott and had one daughter. (2) Elaine born about 1932 she married Charles Greenburg, and had two sons and one daughter. (3) Norma born 10 July 1938, she married Marshall Willis (Sonny) Starr on 17 April 1954 and they had four daughters. (4) Richard Stanley born 19 August 1935 at Cherry Lane, North Carolina. He married two times Janice Emma Spicer and had two daughters. He then married Elaine Esterline Hope and had one daughter. (5) Gerald born 23 November 1943, he married Peggy Earlene Bond, they have no children.

Bert and Carrie moved to Iowa at the time Lynn and Effie did along with other member of the Hendrix family. Bert did farming and carpenter work while living in Iowa. The family lived in Iowa from 1929 to 1934. They had two children there. Lynn and Effie lived there a while after Bert and Carrie moved. Some of the Hendrex family lived out their lives in Iowa and their descendants still live there, others moved to California.

In 1934 Bert's family moved back to North Carolina. Some time after World War II started the family moved to Bel Air, Maryland (family members think it was about 1938). They moved so Bert would have work, there were very few jobs in the mountains of North Carolina at that time.

A quote from Elaine, Bert's oldest daughter, "While living in North Carolina, I was about four years old, I can remember my mother Carrie, Aunt Effie, Aunt Liza and all us children going into the woods to pick galax leaves to be sold to the florist."

Bert was a very good carpenter and was able to find work in Maryland. He and Carrie spent the rest of their lives in Maryland.

Bert was getting ready to build a new house when he became sick with cancer. Bert was never able to build that last house he had planned. He, Carrie and son Gerald lived in a trailer on the land where he had planned to build the house. He even built the foundation for the house before he became to sick to work. Bert's sons-in-law Charles and Sonny had to tear down the foundation after Bert died.

Carrie had to start working while Bert was ill, she had a hard time making ends meet. She worked in a sewing factory making London Fog rain coats.

When Bert died his youngest son, Gerald was about sixteen years old. Carrie had to work to support herself and Gerald. She had to send Gerald to high school. She and Gerald continued to live in the trailer. After Gerald was married the trailer caught on fire and burned. She stayed with her oldest daughter Elaine and her husband, Charles, for a while after the mobile home burned. Norma and her husband Sonny had bought a house and built three apartments near it. Carrie later moved into one of the apartments, that way she had her own place, but was still near one of her daughters.

Carrie's children gave her a surprise birthday party for her eightieth birthday. It turned out to be the highlight of her life, being surrounded by her children, grandchildren and nieces and nephews. Carrie was a widow for about thirty years. When she died she was buried beside Bert.

VERDIE (VERD) ALICE[9] STAMPER, (John (Ander) Andrew[8]), (Troy[7]), (Hiram H.[6]), (John[5]), (Jonathan Jr.[4]), (Jonathan Sr.[3]), (Powell[2]), (John[1]) the third child of John Ander (Andrew) Stamper and Mary Emiline Blevins. She was born 1 May 1902, died 31 May 1972, she is buried at the Cherry Lane Baptist Church Cemetery, Cherry Lane, North Carolina. She married James (Paul) Miles, the son of John Miles and Mary McBride Miles. Paul was born 31 August 1900 and died 16 June 1982. Paul was a good banjo picker and played country and bluegrass music. When he was young he had some of his music recorded. He is buried beside Verdie. The church graveyard where they are buried is less then a mile from where they spent their married life and raised their family.

Virdie and Paul's children are: (1) Vernon Carroll born 22 August 1922 and died 3 March 1944; (2) Wade, born about 1924 and died June 15, 1988; (3) James (Jim), (His grave marker in Italy says James Paul Jr), he was born 25 March 1926 and died May 1946; (4) William Earl (Bill) born 12 March 1929; (5) Mary Lou born 19 March 1931; (6) John Thomas (Tom) born 24 October 1933; (7) Peggy born 24 October 1938; (8) Patsy (Pat) born 25 December 1940; (9) Nancy born 26 September 1942; There was a miscarriage of twins.

STAMPER FOOTPRINTS

The following was written by Nancy Miles Royal. "Mama and Daddy raised us all up to know right from wrong. Mama always stayed home and did her housework. Daddy worked for the State of North Carolina taking care of the school buses of Alleghany, he retired from the State job. We have always been a close family and helped each other in many ways. When any of us need any thing we know that there is someone who will lend a helping hand. Being from a big family has some advantages.

"I (Nancy) am writing this, and I want you to know that I have crippling arthritis. All my brothers and sisters have been so good to me. I could never thank them for all they have done.

My husband Willie has stood by me, if it were not for his loving care I would not be able to live at home. He does the cooking and house work. I can feed myself but that is about all I can do for myself. (Willie died 21 May 1994.)

May God richly bless each one of them. I am glad and thank God that we are all christians saved by the grace of God."

When Verd and Paul celebrated their fiftieth wedding anniversary one of their daughters asked, Verdie's niece, Betty Stamper Latham to bake the cake, and she was honored to do it.

Verd, like her brothers, loved to fish. One winter when her brothers were in Florida she joined them to do some fishing. She was like the other Stampers in that she was always ready go some place new and different. She was a loving kind women, a good friend and neighbor. She was the oldest girl in the family, the big sister, the family often turned to. She was a good friend to her brothers and sisters and always there when they needed her help in and way.

I never did learn how Aunt Verd could do it but she could draw fire from a burn. She would very gently rub her finger over a burn and whisper something and the burn would stop burning and hurting. She did this for me a couple of times when I was a child, and it worked. Maybe it was faith on both parties part.

She was good at sewing and made a lot of her girls dresses. I remember she made some dresses for me and my sister. She was one of the best cooks around, makes no difference when someone stopped in she would always have something good cooked.

She never stopped grieving for her two sons who were killed in World War II. In her later years she was not well, and she was in pain a lot. Verdie left her footprints in Cherry Lane, North Carolina.

VERDIE ALICE STAMPER
AGE 16 YEARS

MINNIE INEZ (INE)[9] STAMPER, (John (Ander) Andrew[8]), (Troy[7]), (Hiram H.[6]), (John[5]), (Jonathan Jr.[4]), (Jonathan Sr.[3]), (Powell[2]), (John[1]) was the fourth child of John Ander (Andrew) Stamper and Mary Emiline Blevins born 16 May 1904, died 25 April 1969. She married John (Raymond) Miles, son of John and Mary McBride Miles, and brother of Paul Miles. Ine's sister Virdie married Paul Miles. Raymond was born 15 October 1904 and died 6 July 1963. They were married on 3 January 1923. Raymond was a Baptist minister and preached at Cherry Lane Baptist Church, Cherry Lane, North Carolina.

Inez and Raymond had five Children: (1) Margaret Louise Miles born 25 December 1923, she married Samuel Clifton Evans 11 May 1941 and they had three children. (2) John Raymond Miles Jr. born 23 May 1926 and died 25 June 1986. He married Earlene Joines on 11 September 1943 and they had four children. (3) Anna Mae Miles born 14 February 1931. She married Clifton (Dillon) Edwards, on 6 May 1950 and they had two children. (4) Walter (Lloyd) Miles born 21 December 1934 and died 22 November 1993. He married Lucille (Ellen) Evans on 29 December 1956, they had two children. (5) Charles (Roy) Miles born 2 February 1938 and died 8 August 1966. Roy was retarded, he was childlike and very loveable. He was a comfort to his mother in her later years. Inez worried that she might die before him, but that was not the case. He died quietly in his sleep at the age of twenty-eight.

The following is a quote from Nancy Miles Royal, a niece of Inez. "Before Inez and her sister Virdie were married they went to Winston-Salem, North Carolina and got a job at R.J.Reynolds Tobacco Co. They had a room in a boarding house of a women named Jordan. Years later after they had moved back to Alleghany County, and were married, Mrs. Jordan would ride the Greyhound bus up the mountain to visit them.

Aunt Inez had really bad headaches, and she would tie an old rag tightly around her head, she said that helped the pain. In her older years she stopped having those headaches.

She was a jolly happy person and seemed happy being a housewife, doing work around the house and having people in to visit. After church services on Sunday she would have a big dinner for her family. There would always be friends and maybe a visiting preacher at the dinner table. She had a big dining room, with a big table, that would seat at least twelve people. The dinning room was used only on Sunday or if she had company. Never did I see her angry. She loved to laugh and enjoyed life. I loved her very much."

The things I remember about Aunt Ine are: She was a kind loving Christian women. She was always helpful to her extended family and friends. She was a great cook, and when I was a child, I loved to visit her, because she would always offer me something good to eat. She had a big garden and canned hundreds of jars of food each year. She would show me the rows and rows of mason jars of fruits and vegetables. She had a milk cow or two and churned the cream to make butter. She made homemade cottage cheese too, which was so delicious, much better then store bought cottage cheese. There was a spring house where she kept the milk, butter and cheese. It was always so nice and cool in the spring house in the summer time. She could sew and crotchet, those were things I wanted to learn to do too. She was a good role model for me.

The years I was ten to about fifteen I would visit her often and we would set and talk. We would watch Roy play while we talked. She always seemed interested in what I had to say, and that made me feel good.

Inez was one of the kind of people who is loved my everyone who knew her, for she gave of her time and self, without any expectations of any thing in return. Inez left her footprints in the area of the Cherry Lane community and the memories of those who knew and loved her.

Inez, Raymond and Roy are buried in the cemetery at Cherry Lane Baptist Church, Cherry Land, North Carolina about one mile off State Highway 21.

BACLE W.[9] STAMPER, (John (Ander) Andrew[8]), (Troy[7]), (Hiram H.[6]), (John[5]), (Jonathan Jr.[4]), (Jonathan Sr.[3]), (Powell[2]), (John[1]) was a twin, he had a twin sister Macle, they were born 24 July 1912. They were the sixth and seventh children of John Ander and Mary Emiline Blevins Stamper. Bacle was a taller and heavier built man than his brothers. Bacle's Indian ancestry showed up just enough to make him a very handsome man. He had an outgoing personality and was a very likeable person.

He married Hazel Royal, she was the daughter of Franklin Royal and Sally (Jane) Brown Royal. She was born on 10 September 1917. Bacle and Hazel had three children. The oldest (1) Herman born on 22 March 1935, at Cherry Lane, North Carolina. At the time of Herman's birth, Bacle and Hazel were living next door to Bacle's brother, Onley and his wife Elizabeth (Liza). Hazle and Elizabeth each had their first child one day apart. With Doctor Bert Choate driving the ten miles from town in his old Model A Ford to deliver their babies. Hazel said, "I had my first labor pain just as I heard the doctor drive away from Onley and Liza's house". Herman married Naydean Hall, they had three children; (a) Mary Jane, born February 1956; (b) Gary, born 1957; and (b) David, born 1967. Bacle and Hazel's next child (2) Wanda born 12 February 1938. Wanda married Henry Proffit and they had three children; (a) Kay, born August 1956; (b) Pam, born September 1957; and (c) Penny, born February 1967. Bacle and Hazle had another daughter, (3) Mary Jane born on 1 September 1947 she died at birth.

Bacle was a superb carpenter, one of the first things he built was a house for his mother, when he was eighteen years old.

He was a building contractor. He was well known for the excellent quality of his work. He lived and ran his building business near Galax, Virginia. His son Herman worked with him and took over the business when Bacle was no longer able to work.

Bacle, like his brothers, liked to travel. In the late 1930's and early 40's he also lived and worked in Maryland. His mother lived with him some of the time when he was in Maryland. She did not like to live alone, but the main reason was she watched after Bacle and Hazel's two children so Hazel could work.

Hazel worked for Roses department stores until she retired after working over twenty years.

Bacle, died 26 May 1991, and is buried at Mount Caramel Baptist Church Cemetery near Roaring Gap, North Carolina. He left his footprints in the lovely homes he built.

HOUSE BUILT BY BACLE STAMPER WHEN HE WAS EIGHTEEN YEARS OLD
(for his mother Mary Blevins Stamper Smith)

BACLE AND HAZLE ROYALL STAMPER
(taken April 1983)

MACLE^{9} STAMPER, (John (Ander) Andrew^{8}), (Troy^{7}), (Hiram H.^{6}), (John^{5}), (Jonathan Jr.^{4}), (Jonathan Sr.^{3}), (Powell^{2}), (John^{1}) was a twin, Bacle was her twin brother. They were the sixth and seventh children of John Ander and Mary Emiline Blevins Stamper and were born on 24 July 1912. Macle is a very beautiful women her dark hair is now a lovely gray and her blue eyes sparkle when she smiles.

Macle has always been a good neighbor. She is a Christian and was very active in her church until her older years, when she became to ill to get out much. All her nieces and nephews only have good things to say about her and all say that they love her very much.

Macle said when she was about eleven years old she went to West Virginia and lived for a year with her Uncle Harry (Monroe) Stamper and his wife Elizabeth (Kattie).

She married Marshal Shore 26 June 1929, she was sixteen when she married. Marshal was a farmer and had a farm in Yadkinville, North Carolina. Like Macle's Stamper ancestors they were tobacco farmers. Macle worked along with Marshal in the tobacco fields. The way the tobacco was planted had improved from the way Powell and Mary did it but not that much. It was still back breaking work to pull off and kill the green tobacco worms. Pull off the sprouts from the side of the stalks called suckers. In the fall the tobacco still had to be graded and packed by hand. Macle would help work in the fields until almost noon and then Marshal would drive her to the house so she could cook a large meal for the family and hired hands.

Marshal and Macle had four sons; (1) Russell born 1931, he married Candy Hive, from Japan, they had no children, and are divorced. He then married Ethel Beoman they had no children. Russell died the fall of 1994. (2) John born 23 December 1936, he married Edith Scott, had three children. John is a Baptist preacher. (3) Charles born 23 October 1940, he married Betty Myrcys, they had two children. (4) Vernon born 20 July 1949, he married Judith Brown, they had four children, one died as a child.

Macle's health was not good at a young age, she had arthritis and was diabetic. She was like all the Stampers in as much as she likes to travel. She made several trips by airplane to California to see her sister Irene. That was several years ago before Irene moved from California, so she could be near Macle.

After Marshal's death 15 December 1969, Macle sold the farm. She had herself a nice little house built near the road, that is were she lives, at this time.

IRENE STAMPER MOORE GILBUENA AND FOUR DAUGHTERS
(back row: Diane, Loretta. and Mires)
(front row: Irene and Becky)

IRENE LAURA[9] STAMPER, (John (Ander) Andrew[8]), (Troy[7]), (Hiram H [6]), (John[5]), (Jonathan Jr.[4]), (Jonathan Sr.[3]), (Powell[2]), (John[1]) was the eighth child of John Ander and Mary Emiline Blevins Stamper. She was born 15 March 1920. She was only nine months old when her father died.

Irene took after her mother in looks, she is a beautiful women with a permanent tan without the sun, her eyes are blue and she has dark hair. She is more slender then her sisters were. She takes good care of herself, she acts and looks younger than her years. Irene married two times first to Marvin Moore who was the father of her children. Marvin was born on 24 July 1916 in Indiana. After their daughters were grown Irene and Marvin divorced.

Irene lived with her brother Onley and his wife Elizabeth at various times before her marriage. At one time she lived with them in Maryland when Onley was working on a farm. There was an old rooster who would chase people and Irene was afraid of him. I was four years old at the time and I loved my Aunt Irene, I wanted to go everywhere she went. I wanted to be like her, because she was so pretty. I am sure I made a pest of myself and she was glad when she could slip away without me following.

When Irene married Marvin Moore, he was in the Army, it was just before World II. She had meet him when she was staying with friends at Low Gap, North Carolina. He was on leave from Fort Bragg, and had gone home with one of his friends for a visit. While Marvin was in the war Irene lived near her family in Maryland or North Carolina. She lived near the army bases when he was in the United States.

She had their first daughter while he was in the Army. After World War II, he got out of the Army and they lived in Englewood, California. After their children were grown they divorced.

They had four daughters; Loretta Louise was born 22 January 1941. She married Jerry Ray DeBinder they had two sons Bryan Ray and Gregory Scott. They live in California. (2) Diane born 31 Jan 1947 she married Len Nichols and had a daughter Bridgett. Diane still lives in California.(3) Meris was born 24 October 1952. She married Randall Arbgast and they have two sons, Jared Brent and Aaron Lynn. Meris and her family moved from California to North Carolina to be near her mother. (4) Rebecca Angela born on 18 January 1957. After she moved with her mother and Steve from California to North Carolina, she married John William Collins Jr. and they had two children, John Michael and Haley Brooke.

Irene would visit her family in North Carolina every year or two and that gave the family an excuse to have a family reunion. The sisters and brothers in the family visited each other sometimes, but the whole family with all the nieces and nephews did not get together until Irene came home. Everyone was excited when they heard that Irene and her girls were coming for a visit.

While Irene and Marvin were married, my family and I visited their family several times over the years, when we lived in California. They visited us when we lived at Fort Ord, California.

Shortly after her divorce Irene married Steve Gilbuena. A few years after she and Steve married they moved from California back to North Carolina. Irene said she lived forty years in California. Irene missed her family in North Carolina and she did want to spend time with her sister Macle. She and Steve have a house near her sister Macle and they see each other almost every day.

The past few years, my sister Shirley and I have visited our Aunts Irene and Macle several times. I have always enjoyed these visits. I have learned a lot about my grandparents from them.

EVA (FAYE)^9 HANKS, (Louella^8 Richardson), Nancy (Nalie)^7 Choate), (Margaret (Peggy)^6 Fender), (Martha^5 Toliver) (Frances (Frankie)^9 **STAMPER**), (Jonathan Sr.^{3}), (Powell^2), (John^1) was the fourth child of Robert Hanks and Loulla Richardson Hanks. She was born on 20 February 1912 and died the summer of 1993. She married Major A. Blevins in 1929. Major's parents were Felix (Quincy) Blevins and Emma Combs Blevins. Major was born on 17 February 1911 and died the winter of 1963.

Major Blevins and Faye Hanks Blevins had six children. One son Ralph Earl born 22 November 1929 and died 15 April 1938. Their daughters are: (1) Carol born 1931; (2) Emogene born 1934; (3) Doris Ann born 17 January 1937; (4) Nancy born 1945, she married two times, her first husband Paul Phipps Wright he was diabetic and died of cancer. He died very young he and Nancy had two sons, Christopher Paul and Samuel David. After Paul's death she married Dr. Gale Jackson (Jack) Ashley, he adopted the sons. (5) Linda Louella born 16 January 1947, she is married but has no children. She is a registered nurse[7].

Major Blevins was the second cousin of the children of John Ander Stamper and Mary Emiline Blevins Stamper from the Blevins side of the family. Felix (Quincy) Blevins who was the father of Major Blevins was Mary Emiline Blevins Stamper's nephew.

JAMES J.^{9} STAMPER, (Mattie Mae^8 Stamper), (Joseph Samuel^7), (Joshua Jr.^{6}), (Joshua Sr.^{5}), (Jonathan Jr.^{4}), (Jonathan Sr.^{3}), (Powell^2), (John^1) was the son of Mattie Mae Stamper and Harlow Stamper. He lives in Independence, Virginia. James married Ruby Luried Wooten and had two children, a daughter and son. (1) His daughter is Shelby Jean, she married Dwain Hale. (2) His son is Roger Stamper, he lives in Surry County, North Carolina.

James has been active in genealogy research for many years and has written several books from his research. He is a good fiddle player and has won first place at the Fiddlers Convention in Galax, Virginia. His son Roger plays the fiddle with him some times and

taught, his paintings are quite good. James helped to build the first library in Independence Virginia. The library was a small log building. James has contributed much to the community and is known for his research and fiddle playing.

JAMES J, STAMPER
(taken November 1993)

WILLIAM HARRISON[9] STAMPER, (Abraham[8]), (Masterson (Bad Mat)[7]), (Jean (Jennie)[6]), (Joshua[5]), (Jonathan Jr.[4]), (Jonathan Sr.[3]), (Powell[2]), (John[1]) was the son of Abraham Stamper and Ruth Emaline------Stamper. He was born on 25 May 1889 and died 1 September 1957. William is buried in White Top Virginia, along with his wife and several children who died young.

William Harrison Stamper married Mary (Polly) Barker about 1913. They had nine children: (1) Roy Lee born 2 August 1914 and died 27 March 1918, he is buried at White top, Virginia. (2) William (Worth) born 20 March 1916 at White Top, Virginia. He married Rosa Zonia Shepard 21 August 1937, his second wife was Orphie Susan Farmer. (3) Mary Ruth born on 7 December 1917 and died on 17 January 1918. (4) Robert Paul was born on 26 March 1919 and died on 17 April 1919. (5) Warren Lincoln born on 14 March 1921 and died on 26 February 1989. Warren married Helen (Thelma) Adams on 14 December 1946. (6) Durphy McKinley born on 24 February 1923 and died the same day. (7) Claude Lee born on 13 June 1924 and died 3 August 1974. Claude married Dessie Blevins about 1944. (8) Thomas Aaron born on 4 September 1926 and died 23 July 1990. Thomas married Helen Hart. (9) Elsie Bertie born on 31 May 1928, at White Top, Virginia. she is still living at the time of this writing.

CHAPTER 10

TENTH GENERATION

BETTY SUE [10] STAMPER, (Onley[9]), (John (Ander) Andrew[8]), (Troy[7]), (Hiram H.[6]), (John[5]), (Jonathan Jr.[4]), (Jonathan Sr.[3]), (Powell[2]), (John[1]) is the oldest daughter of Onley Eugene Stamper and Elizabeth Etta Shaw Stamper. She was born 21 March 1935 at Cherry Lane, North Carolina. The house where she was born still stands about one and half miles from where she now lives. She eloped at the age of sixteen, and married George Henry Latham in Chester, South Carolina 10 July 1951.

George was born 13 January 1931 in Ohio, he is the thirteenth child of Jesse Thomas Latham and Carrie Louise Henry Latham of Chestertown, Maryland. Jesse was the only child of John T. Latham and Sallie R. Biggs Latham. He was born on 24 September 1890, in Chestertown, Maryland. Carrie was the daughter of William T. Henry and Anna Rebecca Stanley Henry. She was born on 16 March 1892 in Chestertown, Maryland. Carrie's mother Anna was her father William's second wife, he was much older then Anna. They had three children; (a) Lottie, (b) Carrie and (c) William. We have no records of William T. Henry's first family. Jesse and Carrie were married in October 1908. Jesse worked most of his adult life in paper mills. The family of Jesse and Carrie moved often in order for Jesse to find work.

When George and Betty eloped he was in the Army, it was the time of the Korean's War. Betty and George were married just sixty-three days when he went to Korea. Betty spent about two months with George's sisters, the rest of the time George was in Korea she spent with her parents. Her mother was devastated when they eloped. At the time Betty knew how her Mother had been hurt and was sorry for the pain she had caused her. She hoped that spending that year with her parents would prepare them for the time she would have to leave them to be with her husband.

After a year in Korea, George was transferred to Japan and Betty joined him there. At the age of seventeen she took a train from Columbus, Ohio to Seattle, Washington, which took three days. From Seattle she took a ship for a ten day trip to Japan. She kept a daily log of that trip which she sent to her mother. After her mother's death, she found the log. Betty and George stayed in Japan for one year.

The year they were in Japan was like a year's honeymoon. They went out to the NCO Club at least ounce a week, they would have dinner, dance and watch the floor show. They went to play bingo about ever week. They also made several friends, whom they went sight seeing over Japan with. They had a house cleaner who came in twice a week to clean the house. This gave Betty time to explore Japan, while George worked, she went by bus and train.

Betty and George had four children and also raised a son who came to live with them as a foster child: (1) Thomas Jacques born 27

October 1953 at Fort Lee, Virginia. He married Deborah Kay Pettry, 6 June 1971, they have one daughter Christina (Tina). (2) Henry Eugene (Gene) born 26 June 1955 at Beale Air Force Base, California. He married Deborah Black Mc Masters 29 October 1981, they had no children, she had two children Candida and Garrett, Gene was a father to them. (3) Georgia Sue born 7 May 1956 at Beale Air Force Base, California. She married three times; Roger Lewis Pilkins, the father of her daughter, Virginia Lorraine; Carmon Seymour and Stephen Lowell Koury. She graduated from Medical school May 1986. (4) David Rodney born 30 September 1965 at Fort Ord, California. (5) Sandy O'Neal Hammack born 29 May 1966, Danbury, North Carolina. He was ten years old when he came to live with the family. He married Susan Elizabeth Hilbert 8 September 1989 in Englewood, Florida. George was the best man at Sandy and Susan's wedding, he was honored that Sandy had asked him.

George stayed in the Army until 1 January 1969. Betty somehow felt she was in the Army too and always says, "The years we were in the Army". During those seventeen years they lived in Maryland three different times, Japan, Virginia two different times, North Carolina, California two different times, Oklahoma, Alaska, Georgia and Germany. The last year George was in the Army he spent in Viet Nam.

While George was in Viet Nam, Betty went to North Carolina and had a house built. The land where the house was built is a three and a half acre plot which was once part of a large boundary of several hundred aches owned by Betty's grandfather John A. Shaw and his sons. It is on Shawtown Road in the Cherry Lane Community of Alleghany County. They lived there for eighteen years before moving to Maryland.

Betty often felt restless during the years they lived in North Carolina. It was an aching hurt to see all the places that she had never seen. That is why money that should have been used for fixing up the house or even education for the children was often spent to take a trip. She knew that her father and uncles always liked to travel and said she had inherited the wanderlust from them.

While living in North Carolina Betty and George both went back to school. When George went back to school he studied computer programming. This turned out to be a good choice for him, as he has had an enjoyable and profitable second career. Betty took a class for Practical Nursing and got her license in 1974. She went to work for Alleghany County Memorial Hospital, in Sparta, North Carolina, right after receiving her license.

Betty was a Licensed Practical Nurse for almost eighteen years before going back to school. While living in Lexington Park, Maryland she went to Charles County Community College and took the Associates Degree course to get her Registered Nurse's license in June 1990. After Betty received her Registered Nurse's license she worked in the Critical Care Unit of St Mary's Hospital in Leonardtown, Maryland for three years before moving back to North Carolina. Also she was a Hospice volunteer in St Mary's County, Maryland.

Betty likes all arts and crafts. At various times she has taken art classes, both oil and water color. She has sold a few oil paintings and some pencils sketches. Photography is another hobby of hers. In the spring of 1971 she took her first cake decorating class and really fell in love with cake decorating. To date Betty has baked all her children's and her granddaughter's wedding cakes. She enjoys baking and decoration cakes for her friends and at one time she baked cakes to sale. Also she taught cake decoration for Wilkes Community College and at a Ben Franklin store in North Carolina.

She has always loved to cook and try out new recipes. She enjoys very much to have the opportunity to cook for guests. When she fixes a meal for others, she feels that she is giving of herself. Some people are feeders and that is what she is, "A Feeder." There is a feeling of nurturing when fixing a meal and serving family and friends. Maybe it is a southern hospitably thing, in any case it gives Betty pleasure to feed people.

Her latest hobby is spinning. In the spring of 1991 she bought a spinning wheel and learned to spin. She has made several things from her Samoyed dogs hair. Family members like to receive gifts made from the soft silky hair of a pet they love. The family has had Samoyed dogs since George got out of the Army. They got their first Samoyed in 1969.

Betty and George became interested in genealogy and have spent the past several years looking up family histories. They have done research in state archives, county courthouses, the National Archive in Washington, visited grave yards, written numerous letters and interviewed many family members.

They lived in Maryland for seven years and four months before moving back to their house in North Carolina to retire. They have moved twenty-four times in the forty-three years they have been married. After all that moving they still enjoy traveling. They are both looking forward to doing a lot of traveling after retirement. Their latest trip was to Australia December 1993.

Betty is working part time in the Critical Care Unit at Twin Counties Regional Community Hospital in Galax, Virginia.

She wants to spend as much time with her sister Shirley as she can. They have not been able to spend much time together over the years and are looking forward to doing so now.

GEORGE AND BETTY STAMPER LATHAM AND THEIR CHILDREN
(David, Gene, George, Betty, Georgia, Tom, and Sandy)
(taken 28 August 1993)

OLEN AND SHIRLEY STAMPER HARRIS AND FAMILY

Left to right: son John and wife Teresa, son Mark and his bride Kim, Shirley, Olen and in front granddaughter Jeana, daughter of John and Teresa.

SHIRLEY JEAN[10] STAMPER, (Onley[9]), (John (Ander) Andrew[8]), (Troy[7]), (Hiram H.[6]), (John[5]), (Jonathan Jr.[4]), (Jonathan Sr.[3]), (Powell[2]) the second daughter of Onley Eugene Stamper and Elizabeth Etta Shaw Stamper was born 25 June 1938 in Churchville, Maryland. She married Olen Vaughn Harris on 28 September 1956, soon after her graduation from high school. They had two sons, John Daniel and Mark Vaughn.

Olen is the son of Thomas Walter Neal Harris and Lura Cynthia Cleary Harris. Thomas was born 26 August 1893 in Alleghany County, North Carolina. Lura was born 12 July 1901 in Alleghany County, North Carolina. Thomas and Lura had six children: (1) Bertha Mae, (2) General Bert, (3) Mary Lou, (4) Olen Vaughn, (5) Mabel, and (6) Bonnie (Sue). Olen was born in Alleghany County, North Carolina, 4 April 1936. Olen is a carpenter he has helped build many houses in Alleghany County. He is a good guitar player and vocalist, he sang and played with the "Christian Quartet", they had several LPs recorded in the 1980s. He plays Bluegrass music, he plays at church and various social gatherings.

Shirley Stamper Harris is a beautiful slender women with blond hair and the bright sparkling blue eyes that some of the Stampers have. Her skin is naturally fair but she seems to always have a tan, as she spends a lot of time outside in the sun both summer and winter. She cares about her health. She exercises several times a week, priding herself on keeping slim.

The most important things in Shirley's life have been her family and church. She is a Christian and lives the christian life every day. A quote from a book she wrote, "Roses Beyond the Sunset", "My job objective, is to obtain a position for the service to my fellowman." She has been able to find just that sort of job. At this time she is working with a program call CAP as a Home Health Aide though the logical hospital.

Shirley worked with the Boy Scouts, when her sons were in scouting. She has been a Sunday School teacher for more then twenty years. She has held various offices in her Church. She did volunteer work in a local Nursing Home. After her father died she helped to look after her mother for twenty three years. She is helping care for her mother-in-law, who needs more care all the time.

Besides being a housewife, mother, caring for her home and gardening, she worked outside the home. Right out of high school she started working for Hanes Knitwear, in Sparta, North Carolina, she worked there for twenty-one years. At Hanes Knitwear, she mostly did sewing, the last year or so she worked as training instructor. She worked for a few years at Meadowbrook Manor Nursing Home. She also worked at chicken farming for about six years. At the time of this writing Shirley works for CAP, a home health program where she takes care of patients in their own home.

Shirley, also enjoys traveling, she and Olen have taken several trips. In the future she, Olen, Betty and George hope to travel some together. They have had the opportunity to take two trips together. One to see their children who live in the Norfolk, Virginia area. Another with two other couples to Ohio, which was a fun trip.

Shirley's hobbies include Bible study, travel, cooking, bowling, gardening, taking pictures and writing. She enjoys spending time with her grandchildren. The summer of 1990 she had a book published, about her Christian life, entitled "Roses Beyond The Sunset".

INA GRACE^{10} STAMPER, (Linville Kemp^{9}), (John (Ander) Andrew^{8}), (Troy^{7}), (Hiram H.^{6}), (John^{5}), (Jonathan Jr.^{4}), (Jonathan Sr.^{3}), (Powell^{2}), (John^{1}) the daughter of Linville Kemp and Effie Hendrix Stamper, was born 4 May 1925 in Iowa. She died 13 September 1974, while having surgery to have a brain tumor removed at the Baptist Hospital in Winston-Salem, North Carolina.

Ina Grace married Earnest Brackins 12 September 1942, he is a Minister. Ina grace and Earnest had four children: (1) Elsie B. was born 23 March 1944. She married Martin Bruce Chadwick they had two children. (2) William Kemp Brackins was born 23 April 1945. He married two times, to Patricia do not have last name and Rosemary Phipps. Do not know how many children, at least one son by Rosemary. (3) Phillip Lester was born 27 March 1953. He married Sharon do not have last name, they had two children. (4) Christopher Neal was born 9 January 1956. He married Diane, do not have last name, and they had one child.

VIRGINIA^{10} STAMPER, (Linville Kemp^{9}), (John (Ander) Andrew^{8}), (Troy^{7}), (Hiram H.^{6}), (John^{5}), (Jonathan Jr, ^{4}), (Jonathan Sr.^{3}), (Powell^{2}), (John^{1}) the daughter of Linville Kemp And Effie Hendrix Stamper was born 27 July 1927 in Iowa. She married Hugh Perry they had seven children, two died as infants.

Virginia and Hugh's other children are: (1) Ronnie who was born 5 December 1946. He married Norma Bell, they have one child. (2) Dennie he was born 16 December 1948. He married Ann Heart they had two children, Sammy and Missy. (3) Reggie was born 4 December 1952. He married twice, first Sandra Poole and had one son Jamie. His second wife was Cindy Cox and they had three children. (4) Allen was born 14 June 1954. He married Sherry Parsons and they had three children, Shawn, Joshua and April. (5) Lou Ann, born 18 November 1958. She married Freddie Roberts and they had two children Stacy and Crystal.

Virginia and Hugh Perry divorced. On 20 January 1974, Virginia married Frank Hendrix. Virginia and Frank reside near Sparta, North Carolina. Virginia works at the Sparta Florist.

JOHN EDWARD[10] STAMPER, (Linville Kemp[9]), (John (Ander) Andrew[8]), (Troy[7]), (Hiram H.[6]), (John[5]), (Jonathan Jr.[4]), (Jonathan Sr.[3]), (Powell[2]), (John[1]) the son of Linville Kemp and Effie Hendrix Stamper was born in Iowa 24 March 1930. He married Cora Mae Ramey 7 October 1951. Cora Mae was born 12 May 1933. They had four children, two boys and two girls. (1) Pamela S. was born 13 August 1954. She married Lars Erik Brandt who is from Sweden. They have two sons, Erik (Cory) and Edward (Erik). (2) Bennett Lynn (Bennie) he was born 4 March 1957. (3) Shannon she was born 1 September 1962, she is a stewardess for US Airlines. (4) John Edward was born 3 June 1972.

John owns his own business and his sons Bennie and John Edward help him run it. It is a family business with Cora Mae doing the book work. They install septic tanks and do maintenance on them.

John and Cora Mae live in Mount Airy, North Carolina and have a beautiful mountain home where they spend a lot of time in the summer. They are interested in the history of the Stamper Family. Cora Mae has helped with research of the Stampers.

LONZO[10] STAMPER, (Berti (Bert) Schley[9]), (John (Ander) Andrew[8]), (Troy[7]), (Hiram H.[6]), (John[5]), (Jonathan Jr.[4]), (Jonathan Sr, [3]), (Powell[2]), (John[1]) is the oldest child of Bert Schley Stamper and Carrie Ann Hendrex Stamper. He was born on 1 April 1930 in Carson Iowa. He married two times. First to Elsie Gentry on 23 December 1949. She is the daughter of Jesse Gentry and Hazel (do not have her maiden name) Gentry. They had three children: (1) Michael born on 26 July 1951, (2) David born on 18 January 1953, and (3) Larry born on 27 March 1959. They lived in Bel Air, Maryland. Lonzo and Elsie divorced.

Lonzo married Maude Scott in 1965, they had one daughter Judy Michelle on 17 February 1967. They now live in Johnson City, Tennessee.

ELAINE[10] STAMPER, (Berti (Bert) Schley[9]), (John (Ander) Andrew[8]), (Troy[7]), Hiram H.[6]), (John[5]), (Jonathan Jr.[4]), (Jonathan Sr.[3]), (Powell[2]), (John[1]) the daughter of Berti (Bert) Schley Stamper and Carrie Ann Hendrex was born about 1932 in Iowa.

Elaine married Charles Greenburg and they had one daughter and two sons. Charles's job once took him to Brazil and Elaine went with him. She said this was a very good time for her, as she enjoyed travelling.

Charles Greenburg died about 1989 of a myocardial infarction. Elaine was very lonely after Charles' death. She has found comfort in working for her church. She does volunteer work for the community. She likes to travel and takes trips every chance she gets.

Elaine spends time with her children and her sister Norma. Elaine worked for many years in a dentist's office before retiring. She lives in Edgewood, Maryland in the house she and Charles lived in.

RICHARD[10] STAMPER, (Berti (Bert) Schley[9]), (John (Ander) Andrew[8]), (Troy[7]), (Hiram[6]), (John[5]), (Jonathan Jr.[4]), (Jonathan Sr.[3]), (Powell[2]), (John[1]) is the son of Berti (Bert) Schley Stamper and Carrie Ann Hendrex Stamper. He was born on 19 August 1935 in Cherry Lane, North Carolina. He married two times, first to Janice Emma Spicer on 12 May 1957. Janice Emma Spicer was born on 24 November 1937.

Richard and Janice lived in Bristol, Pennsylvania. They had two daughters Linda Gene born on 31 March 1958 and Diane Lee born on 12 March 1960, both were born in Bristol, Pennsylvania.

After Richard and Janice divorced, Richard married Elaine Esterline Hope. Elaine was the daughter of James Hope and Margaret (don't have her maiden name) Hope. Elaine was born on 24 February 1932 in Philadelphia, Pennsylvania. Richard and Elaine had one daughter Carrie Ann born on 7 October 1973 in Bristol, Pennsylvania. They now live in Johnson City, Tennessee.

NORMA[10] STAMPER, (Berti (Bert) Schley[9]), (John (Ander) Andrew[8]), (Troy[7]), (Hiram H.[6]), (John[5]), (Jonathan Jr.[4]), (Jonathan Sr.[3]), (Powell[2]), (John[1]) the daughter of Bert and Carrie Hendrix Stamper was born 10 July 1938. She married Marshall Willis (Sonny) Starr 17 April 1954. They had four children, one son who died as an infant. Their three daughters are: (1) Debbie Mae she was born 29 November 1954. She married Jami Melani on 11 February 1978, they had three sons, (a) Jason Kirk, (b) Jeremy Carl and (c) Joshua Brant, (2) Marsha Karen she was born 18 Jan 1957. She married Paul Thomas Walker on 14 October 1977, they had three sons, (a) Zachery Charles, (b) Travis Evan, and (c) Seth Thomas. (3) Connie Ann she was born 20 August 1858. She married James Joseph Turek on 30 June 1984, they had one son, James Marshall.

Norma and Sonny live in Falston, Maryland. Norma is a great cook and home maker. She gets much pleasure in keeping her house looking great. She helps her husband Sonny with the family business. They own a fleet of school buses and then leases them back to the state of Maryland. Her daughters and grandsons are her greatest joy, she spends as much time as she can with them.

GERALD[10] STAMPER, (Berti (Bert) Schley[9]), (John (Ander) Andrew[8]), (Troy[7]), (Hiram H.[6]), (John[5]), (Jonathan Jr.[4]), (Jonathan[3]), (Powell[2]), (John[1]) is the youngest child of Berti (Bert) Schley Stamper and Carrie Ann Hendrex Stamper. He was born on 23 October 1943 in Belair Maryland. He married Peggy Earlene Bond. Peggy was born on 2 March 1944. Gerald and Peggy have no children at this time.

VERNON MILES

VERNON CARROLL^{10} MILES, (Verdie Alice^{9} **STAMPER**), (John (Ander) Andrew^{8}), (Troy^{7}), (Hiram^{6}), (John^{5}), (Jonathan Jr.^{4}), (Jonathan Sr. ^{3}), (Powell^{2}), (John^{1}) was the oldest child of John Paul Miles and Verdie A.Stamper Miles. He was born 22 August 1922 in Alleghany County, North Carolina. He was killed in action, at sea, near North Africa in World War II, his body was never found. He was only twenty two years old when he was killed.

WADE VAN^{10} STAMPER, (Verdie A.^{9}Stamper), (John (Ander) Andrew^{8}), (Troy^{7}), (Hiram H.^{6}), (John^{5}), (Jonathan Jr.^{4}), (Jonathan Sr.^{3}) (Powell^{2}), (John^{1}) was the second child of John Paul Miles and Verdie A. Stamper miles. He was born 1 February 1924 in Alleghany County, North Carolina. He married Jamalee (Jo) Franklin, on 11 September 1943, they were high school sweethearts. They lived in Rich Hill community, North Carolina. They had three children; (1) Gary Van, (2) Randy, and (3) Angela.

Their son Gary Van was drowned soon after graduating from the eight grade, on 20 June 1959. Wade died 15 June 1988. Jo still lives where she and Wade lived and raised their family.
Her daughter's family lives near her.

JAMES PAUL(JIM)^{10} MILES, (Verdie Alice^{9} **STAMPER**),John (Ander) Andrew^{8}), (Troy^{7}), (Hiram H.^{6}), (John^{5}), (Jonathan Jr.^{4}), (Jonathan Sr.3^{2}), (Powell^{2}), (John^{1}) was the third child of John Paul Miles and Verdie A. Stamper Miles. He was born 25 March 1926 in Alleghany County, North Carolina. He married soon before he was to go in to the Army in World War II, to Arlene Jolly. His daughter was born after he went to Europe. Her name is Jimmy Sue Miles. She was adopted by Earn Hanks and Maye Miles Hanks, who were the Uncle and Aunt of Jim.

Jim was killed in Italy, May 1946, after the end of World War II. He was on his way home when the jeep he was riding in was hit by a train. He is buried in the American Cemetery near Florence, Italy. The name on his grave stone is James Paul Miles Jr. but his family says his name was James Lee Miles. George, Betty and their children visited and put flowers on his grave the summer of 1964.

The cemetery is in a beautiful place. It was very surprising to see that the blue-green mountains look almost the same as the mountains in North Carolina where Jim grew up.

WILLIAM (BILL)^{10} MILES, (Verdie Alice^{9} **STAMPER**,(John (Ander) Andrew ^{8}), (Troy^{7}), (Hiram H.^{6}), (John^{5}), (Jonathan Jr.^{4}), (Jonathan Sr.^{3}), (Powell^{2}), (John^{1}) was the fourth child of John Paul Miles and Verdie A. Stamper Miles. He was born 12 March 1926 in Alleghany County, North Carolina. He married Dorothy Jean Johnson and they had two sons. James and Grey, they are both preachers. Bill and Dorothy live in Statesville, North Carolina.

MARY LOU[10] MILES, (Verdie Alice[9] **STAMPER**), (John (Ander) Andrew[8]), (Troy[7]), (Hiram H.[6]), (John[5]), (Jonathan Jr.[4]), (Jonathan Sr.[3]) (Powell[2]), (John[1]) was the fifth child of John Paul Miles and Verdie A. Stamper Miles. She was born 19 March in Alleghany County, North Carolina. She married Wesley (Herbert) Edwards and they had four children. Herbert died in 1972.

Mary Lou and Herbert's children are; (1) Paula, (2) Pamela, (3) Phil, who is a preacher, and (4) Pattie. Mary Lou has twelve grandchildren. Mary Lou has had to work hard to raise her family.

At the time of this writing Mary Lou lives in Sparta, North Carolina and manages the Alleghany Inn. She is a cheerful outgoing person, and is well liked by all who know her.

JOHN THOMAS (TOM)[10] MILES, (Verdie Alice[9] **STAMPER**), (John Ander[8]), (Troy[7]), (Hiram[6]), (John[5]), (Jonathan Jr.[4]), Jonathan Sr.[3]) (Powell[2]), (John[1]) was the sixth child and youngest son of John (Paul) Miles and Verdie Alice Stamper Miles. He was born in Alleghany County, North Carolina on 24 October 1933. He married Shirley Lee Wagnor on 25 December 1951. They had two children, (1) Annita Lynn born 21 February 1955 and (2) Jody Theodore born 10 January 1967.

The Tom Miles family moved to Irdell County, North Carolina in 1962. Tom worked as a supervisor for a local engineering company for twenty-one years. He is now employed at Suburban Propane Company. Shirley worked as a beauty advisor for Merle Norman Cosmetics twelve years. She is now managing "Ralph Lauren Polo" store. They are proud to say they are a Christian family.

PEGGY[10] MILES, (Verdie Alice[9] **STAMPER**), (John (Ander) Andrew[8]), (Troy[7]), (Hiram H.[6]), (John[5]), (Jonathan Jr.[4]), (Jonathan Sr.[3]), (Powell[2]), (John[1]) was the seventh child of John Paul Miles and Verdie A. Stamper Miles. She was born 24 October 1938 in Alleghany County, North Carolina. She married James Dezern, they had two sons Jeff and Bradley.

Peggy has one step-daughter Karen Dezern. They live in Winston Salem, North Carolina.

PATSY[10] MILES, (Verdie Alice[9] **STAMPER**), (John (Ander) Andrew[8]), (Troy[7]) (Hiram[6]), (John[5]), (Jonathan Jr.[4]), (Jonathan Sr.[3]) (Powell[2]), (John[1]) was the eighth child of John Paul Miles and Verdie A. Stamper Miles. She was born 25 December 1940 in Alleghany County, North Carolina. She first married David Walker and they had two sons Varon and Chris Walker. After their sons were grown Pat and David divorced. Pat is now married to Jim Wyatt. They appear to be having a happy life together.

NANCY[10] MILES, (Verdie (Alice)[9] **STAMPER**), (John (Ander) Andrew[8]), (Troy[7]), (Hiram[6]), (John[5]), (Jonathan Jr.[4]), (Jonathan Sr.[3]), (Powell[2]), (John[1]) was the ninth child of John Paul Miles and Verdie Alice Stamper Miles. She was born 26 September 1942 in Alleghany County, North Carolina. She has a son Vernon Martin (Martie) who changed his name to Royal after Nancy married Willie G. Royal. Nancy married Willie G. Royal in 1966. Nancy let Martie live with her brother Wade and his wife Jo until she married. She and Willie have one daughter Sherry Lydia Royal. Willie has two children from a previous marriage.

Nancy has crippling arthritis, there are a lot of things she can not do for herself. She can hold a pen or pencil and write, her hand writing is lovely and easy to read. She has sent me much of the information about her parents, sisters and brothers.

Nancy's husband Willie G. Royal, died on 21 May 1994 of leukemia. They were married twenty-eight years. A short time before Willie's death their daughter, Sherry, moved back home to help care for her parents. After Willie's death Sherry remained at home to help care for her mother, Nancy.

MARGARET (LOUISE)[10] MILES, (Minnie (Inez)[9] **STAMPER**), (John (Ander) Andrew[8]), (Troy[7]), (Hiram H.[6]), (John[5]), (Jonathan Jr.[4]), (Jonathan Sr.[3]), (Powell[2]), (John[1]) was the oldest child of John (Raymond) Miles and Minnie (Inez) Stamper Miles. She was born 25 December 1923 in Alleghany County, North Carolina. She married Samuel Clifton (Cliff) Evans 11 May 1941. Louise and Cliff made their home near Sparta, North Carolina. They had three children: (1) Margaret Ann, (2) Sandra Lee, and (3) Samuel Clifton Jr.

Cliff was the son of John Henry Evans and Susan Anice Warren Evans. He was born 12 November 1913 in Alleghany County, North Carolina. He traveled west as a young man, he worked in a jewelry store in Yuma, Arizona. He owned Evans Jewelry Store in Sparta, North Carolina for many years and repaired timepieces.

Cliff also had a great interest in country music and played the guitar. After selling the jewelry store he had a clock and watch repair shop across the road from his house.

Louise worked in the jewelry store with Cliff, and she continued to work in the store after it was sold to Sheets. She has a large garden every year and like her mother, cans lots of vegetables. She is an excellent cook and enjoys cooking. She does some cooking for a local restaurant which is managed by her daughter. Louise is very active in the community, working with the American Heart Association as well as other community actives. She is active in her church as well.

She helps to arrange the Stamper reunions each year. The information listed here about her family and the families of her brothers and sister was furnished by Louise Miles Evans.

JOHN RAYMOND[10] MILES, (Minnie Inez[9] **STAMPER**),(John (Ander) Andrew[8]), (Troy[7]), (Hiram H.[6]), (John[5]), (Jonathan Jr.[4]), (Jonathan Sr.[3]), (Powell[2]), (John[1]) was the second child of John (Raymond) Miles Sr. and Minnie(Inez) Stamper Miles. He was born 23 May 1926 in Alleghany County, North Carolina. He married Earlene Joines 11 September 1943 and they had four children; (1) Harold Dean, (2) Larry David, (3) Wanda Lynn, and (4) John (Marty) Martin.

John Raymond (Junior) died 25 June 1986. At this time Earlene works for Alleghany Inn in Sparta, North Carolina.

ANNA MAE[10] MILES, (Minnie (Inez)1[9] **STAMPER**),(John (Ander) Andrew[8]), (Troy[7]), (Hiram H.[6]), (John[5]), (Jonathan Jr.[4]), Jonathan Sr.[3]), Powell[2]), (John[1]) was the fourth child of John (Raymond) Miles and Minnie (Inez) Stamper Miles. She was born 14 February 1931 in Alleghany County, North Carolina. She married Clifton (Dillon) Edwards and they had two children, Shirley Ann and Bobby Dale.

Anna May and Clifton own a farm in Alleghany County, North Carolina. Anna Mae worked in the cafeteria at Alleghany County High School for many years. She now works for Alleghany Inn, Sparta, North Carolina. She is a fun loving person and has always liked to play practical jokes.

WALTER (LLOYD)[10] MILES, (Minnie (Inez)[9] **STAMPER**), (John (Ander) Andrew[8]), (Troy[7]), Hiram H.[6]), (John[5]), (Jonathan Jr.[4]), (Jonathan Sr.[3]), (Powell[2]), (John[1]) was the third child of John (Raymond) Miles and Minnie (Inez) Stamper Miles. He was born 21 December 1934 in Alleghany County, North Carolina. He married Lucille Ellen Evans on 10 May 1956 and they had two children, Michael Wayne and Karen. Lloyd was a barber. He and his family lived in Winston Salem, North Carolina. Lloyd died on 22 November 1993, he is buried at Cherry Lane Union Baptist Church Cemetery. His parents and his brother Roy are buried in the same cemetery.

He owned the house where he grew up, and his family spent many weekends there. The children of Inez and Raymond have been spending Thanksgiving and Christmas there for many years, at the house where they grew up. It is their family reunion time.

Lloyd always enjoyed family reunions, he attended the reunions on both sides of his family. He had an outgoing personality and was well liked by those who knew him. Lloyd left his footprints in Alleghany County and Winston Salem, North Carolina.

HERMAN[10] STAMPER, (Bacle[9]), (John (Ander) Andrew[8]), (Troy[7]), (Hiram H.[6]), (John[5]), (Jonathan Jr.[4]), (Jonathan Sr.[3]), (Powell[2]), (John[1]) is the oldest child of Bacle Stamper and Hazel Royal Stamper. Herman was born on 22 March 1935 in Cherry Lane, North Carolina. He married Naydean Hall. Herman and Naydean had three children, (1) Mary Jane born February 1956, (2) Gary born in 1957, and (3) David born in 1967. After all their children were grown Herman and Naydean divorced.

Herman is a carpenter and building contractor in Galax, Virginia. In addition to his own business he took over his father, Bacle Stamper's business after he retired.

WANDA[10] STAMPER, (Bacle[9]), (John (Ander) Andrew[8]), (Troy[7]), (Hiram H.[6]), (John[5]), (Jonathan Jr.[4]), Jonathan Sr.[3]), (Powell[2]), (John[1]) is the daughter of Bacle Stamper and Hazel Royal Stamper. Wanda was born on 12 February 1938. Wanda married Henry Proffit. Wanda and Henry had three children: (1) Kay was born August 1956, (2) Pam was born September 1957 and (3) was born February 1967.

After Wanda's father, Bacle Stamper, died she moved next door to her mother Hazle so she could look after her, as Hazel's health is not good. They live near Galax, Virginia.

LORETTA LOUISE[10] MOORE, (Irene Laura[9] **STAMPER**), (John (Ander) Andrew[8]), (Troy[7]), (Hiram H.[6]), (John[5]), (Jonathan Jr.[4]), (Jonathan Sr.[3]), (Powell[2]), (John[1]) the oldest child of Irene Laura Stamper Moore and Marvin Moore was born on 22 January 1941 in Mt. Vernon, Illinois. Lorette married Jerry Ray DeBinder. Jerry was born on 1 November 1935. Lorette and Jerry have two sons, Bryan Ray and Gregory Scott. They all live in California.

DIANE[10] MOORE, (Irene Laura[9] **STAMPER**), (John (Ander Andrew [8]), (Troy[7]), (Hiram H.[6]), (John[5]), (Jonathan Jr.[4]), (Jonathan Sr.[3]), (Powell[2]), (John[1]) is the second daughter of Irene Laura Stamper Moore and Marvin Moore. Diane was born on 31 January 1947 in Long Beach, California. Diane married Len Nichols. Len was born about 1942 in Englewood, California. Diane and Len had one daughter Bridgett. Len died sometime after Bridgett was born. Diane lives in California.

MERIS[10] MOORE, (Irene Laura[9] **STAMPER**), (John (Ander) Andrew[8]), (Troy[7]), (Hiram H.[6]), (John[5]), (Jonathan Jr.[4]), (Jonathan Sr.[3]), (Powell[2]), (John[1]) is the third daughter of Irene Laura Stamper Moore and Marvin Moore. Meris was born on 24 October 1952 in Englewood, California. Meris married Randall Arbgast. Randall was born on 13 February 1949. Randall is legally blind. Meris and Randall have two sons, Jared Brent and Aaron Lynn. They moved from California to Yadkinville, North Carolina to be near Meris' mother, Irene.

REBECCA (BECKY) ANGELA[10] MOORE, (Irene Laura[9] **STAMPER**), (John (Ander) Andrew[8]), (Troy[7]), (Hiram H.[6]), (John[5]), (Jonathan Jr.[4]), (Jonathan Sr.[3]), (Powell[2]), (John[1]) is the youngest daughter of Irene Laura Stamper Moore and Marvin Moore. She was born on 18 January 1957 in Los Angles, California. She married John William Collins Jr., he was born on 20 December 1948 in Winston- Salem, North Carolina. Becky and John have two children, John (Michael) and Haley Brooke.

Becky's father Marvin Moore who's health is very bad now, has moved from California to live with Becky's family near Winston-Salem, North Carolina.

WARREN LINCOLN[10] STAMPER, (William Harrison[9]), (Abraham[8]), (Masterson (Bad Mat)[7]), (Jane (Jennie)[6]Stamper), (Joshua Sr.[5]),(Jonathan Jr.[4]), (Jonathan Sr.[3]), (Powell[2]), (John[1]), was the son of William Harrison Stamper and Mary (Polly) Barker Stamper. He was born on 14 March 1921 in White Top, Virginia.

Warren was in the Army during the second World War. Shortly after his discharge from the Army he meet Helen (Thelma) Adams, she was from Konnarock, Virginia. Her parents were Kenny Manuel Adams and Fannie Jane Pennington. Thelma was born on 5 September 1920 in Konnarock, Virginia. Thelma went to a private Lutheran School in Konnarock.

On a beautiful fall day, when White Top mountain was all gold and red, Warren took Thelma for a drive and parked not far from the top, and that is where he proposed marriage. They were married on 14 December 1946. Warren and Thelma had a good life together. They had two sons (1) Michael Warren born on 21 February 1948, he only lived a few weeks, he died on 5 March 1948. They did not have another child for eleven years, so you can imagine their joy when they had another son. (2) Rodney Gene was born 7 December 1959 in Arlington, Virginia. They moved many times and spent many years in northern Virginia. When Warren retired they moved to Sparta, North Carolina and bought a home. After his retirement Warren was sick a lot he had several strokes. Warren died on a cold February day, on 26 February 1989, he is buried in the Sparta Cemetery not far from where he lived. Thelma still lives in their retirement home.

CHAPTER 11

ELEVENTH GENERATION

THOMAS (TOM) JACQUES[11] LATHAM, (Betty Sue[10] **STAMPER**), (Onley[9]), (John (Ander) Andrew[8]), (Troy[7]), (Hiram H.[6]), (John[5]), (Jonathan Jr.[4]), (Jonathan Sr.[3]), (Powell[2]), (John[1]) is the oldest child of Betty Sue Stamper Latham and George Henry Latham. Thomas was born on 27 October 1953 at Fort Lee, Virginia. He was named for his grandfather, Jesse Thomas Latham and a friend of his father's. His father's friend was Robert Victor Jacques. Tom finally met Robert Jacques in 1985.

Thomas Jacques Latham is a 1971 graduate of Alleghany County High School, in Sparta, North Carolina. Shortly after his graduation he married Deborah (Debbie) Kay Pettry of Hillsville, Virginia. Debbie was born 17 May 1953, her parents are James Larry Pettry and Helena (Lena) Belle Alderman Pettry.

Tom joined the United States Air Force about six months after he and Debbie married. He spent almost eight years in the Air Force. Most of the time he was in the Air Force he and his family spent in Biloxi, Mississippi and Hahn, Germany.

After his discharge in 1979 he began his studies with Virginia College of Technology in Blacksburg, Virginia. Debbie worked in a factory, to support the family so he could go to college. He graduated in three years with a Bachelor of Science Degree in Math and a minor in Computer Science. He graduated on 31 August 1982. A week after his graduation he and his family moved to Hollywood, Maryland where he started working for PRB Associates, Inc, as a computer systems analyst. He is still working for the same company, twelve years later. Tom earned a Master's degree in Computer Science from the Florida Institute of Technology in 1989.

Debbie attended Saint Mary's College in Saint Mary's City, Maryland after they moved to Maryland, she graduated May 1987. She now works as a department manager for Leggetts department store in Hollywood, Maryland.

Tom and Debbie have one daughter Christina (Tina) Michelle. She was born on 30 March 1973 at Biloxi, Mississippi. When Tina was three the family moved to Hahn, Germany. Tina went to school for the first two years in Germany. She graduated from Leonardtown high school, Leonardtown, Maryland in May 1991. She is now taking classes at Charles County Community College, in La Plata, Maryland.

Tina married Brian Orr on 28 August 1993 in Hollywood, Maryland. They had a large and very beautiful garden wedding, followed by a fun reception. They make their home in Lexington Park, Maryland. Tina and Brian bought the house Tina's grandparents, George and Betty Stamper Latham, owned while they were living in Maryland.

Tina and Brian are expecting their first child in September 1995.

HENRY (GENE) EUGENE[11] LATHAM, (Betty Sue[10] **STAMPER**), (Onley[9]), (John (Ander) Andrew[8]), (Troy[7]), (Hiram H.[6]), (John[5]), (Jonathan Jr.[4]), (Jonathan Sr.[3]), (Powell[2]), (John[1]) is the second child of Betty Sue Stamper Latham and George Henry Latham. Gene was born on 26 May 1955 at Beale Air Force, Yuba county, Marysville, California. Gene was named for his grandfather Onley Eugene Stamper and his father George Henry Latham.

Gene graduated from Alleghany county high school May 1972. He had earned a National Merit Scholarship and another scholarship from East Carolina University, he went to East Carolina University only one semester. He then joined the United States Air Force. He served in the Air Force for about five years. He spent two of those years in Fulda, Germany.

While stationed in Germany, Gene built a computer from a kit. Here is a quote from, (The Stats and Stripes) newspaper, dated Thursday May 13, 1976: Wasserkuppe, Germany (S&S) "There is a Airman here at this isolated radar station who has an odd roommate. At least it doesn't smoke in bed, keep late hours or drink to much. Airman 1.C. Gene Latham, a radar operator, has as a companion a $600 computer he built himself."

Gene was stationed in San Antonio, Texas, when he got out of the Air Force and he remained there. He got a job with Data Point a computer company, as a computer programmer and systems analyst. He worked for this company for fourteen years. He traveled to Belgium, New Zealand, and Brazil while working for that company.

Gene Latham married Deborah Black Mc Masters on 29 October 1981 in San Antonio, Texas. Deborah had been married before and had two children Candida Mc Masters age seven and Garrett Mc Masters age six. Gene and Deborah had no children together. Gene was a father to Candida and Garrett.

Deborah Black Mc Masters Latham likes theater work and has acted in and directed plays and helped to write plays which were a big success. She loves to cook, does catering, plans weddings and bakes wedding cakes.

Gene gave Candida McMasters away in marriage to Thomas Johnson on 14 May 1994 in San Antonio, Texas. It was a lovely garden wedding. Gene's parents and all his brothers and sister came to the wedding. Candida and Thomas had a baby girl 12 march 1995, she weighted 3 pound and 14 ounces, she was born about seven weeks early. She is doing fine, her name is Savannah Renea Johnson.

Gene and Deborah have a home in San Antonio, Texas and they both have jobs there.

GEORGIA SUE[11] LATHAM, (Betty Sue[11] **STAMPER**), (Onley[9]), (John (Ander) Andrew[8]), (Troy[7]), (Hiram H.[6]), (John[5]), (Jonathan Jr.[4]), (Jonathan Sr.[3]), (Powell[2]), (John[1]) is the third child of Betty Sue Stamper Latham and George Henry Latham. Georgia was born on 7 May 1956 at Beale Air Force Base, Yuba County, California. Georgia Sue was named for her father and mother.

Georgia married Roger Lewis Pilkins on 16 June 1972. He was born 19 August 1953 in West Jefferson, North Carolina. He was a twin, his twin sister was named Genevia. His parents were John Lee Pilkins and Gertrude Mooney Pilkins. The family lived at Mouth of Wilson, Virginia.

Georgia Sue Latham Pilkins and Roger Lewis Pilkins had one daughter, Virginia Lorraine (Lori) Pilkins. Georgia and Roger divorced when Virginia Lorraine (Lori) was a little over three years old. When Virginia Lorraine (Lori) was eighteen years old she had her name changed from Pilkins to Latham. She had been called Lori by the family since she was a baby, at the time she had her name changed to Latham, she wanted to be called Virginia. So now everyone except her grandparents and a few older relatives, call her Virginia.

Georgia raised Virginia Lorraine with the help of a step-father. Roger did not see her again after the divorce, he never helped with child support. Virginia's grandmother Gertrude Mooney Pilkins always sent her gifts at Christmas and for her birthday. At this time Virginia is living with her mother and step-father, Stephen (Steve) Lowell Koury. She is going to college, she is hoping to become a Veterinarian (DVM).

Georgia married Stephen Lowell Koury on 7 August 1982. He is from Philadelphia, Pennsylvania. Steve is the love of her life. He has helped her raise Virginia. He has been supportive in everything she does.

After Georgia and Roger Pilkins divorced she took her maiden name back, Latham. She started back to school and earned her Bachelor of Arts degree from West Chester State University, West Chester, Pennsylvania, in 1980. She graduated Magna Cum Laude and belongs to Psi Chi, an National Honor Society.

It was around the time of her graduation from West Chester State University that she decided she wanted to be a medical doctor. This began many long years of study and hard work. Georgia received a scholarship from the North Carolina Board of Governors for medical school. She graduated from the University of North Carolina School of Medicine, Chapel Hill, North Carolina in May 1986, with the degree of Medical Doctor.

From 1987 to 1991 she worked as a Guest Researcher for the National Institutes of Health, Bethesda, Maryland. Her work included research in Alzheimer's disease and depression in the elderly. At the same time she was working on research for the Department of Behavioral

Biology at Walter Reed Army Institute of Research, Washington, D. C., doing research in Sleep Deprivation. Also during this same time period she was Founder and President of Medical Software Innovations, where she developed software for medical research and practice. In 1991 and 1992, she worked in Diabetes research at Walter Reed Army Medical Center, Washington, D. C., where she worked on research for a new oral medication for diabetes, this medication is now on the market. In 1992, Georgia was recognized by Who's Who Among Rising Young Americans in Society and Business.

Dr. Georgia S. Latham completed a residency in family practice at the Moses H, Cone Family Practice, Greensboro, North Carolina. She is a member of the following professional organizations: American Medical Association, North Carolina Medical Society, American Academy of Family Physicians and North Carolina Academy of Family Physicians.

Today Doctor Georgia Sue Latham is in private practice in Sparta, North Carolina. Her husband Stephen Koury is carpenter. He is working on building them a home in the mountains of Alleghany County, North Carolina.

DAVID RODNEY[11] LATHAM, (Betty Sue[10] **STAMPER**), (Onley[9]), (John (Ander) Andrew[8]), (Troy[7]), (Hiram H.[6]), (John[5]), (Jonathan Jr.[4]), (Jonathan Sr[3]), (Powell[2]), (John[1]) is the fourth child of Betty Sue Stamper Latham and George Henry Latham. He was born at Fort Ord, California, near Monterey in Salinas County on 30 September 1965. The family moved to Alleghany county, North Carolina when David was two years old. They lived there until after David graduated high from college.

David's mother worked most of the time after the family moved to North Carolina and David was cared for during the day by his grandmother, Elizabeth Shaw Stamper. David and his grandmother became very close. She was more then a grandmother, she was, Granny, his second Mom.

The year David was nine years old his parents took him on a trip to Germany for four weeks. His brother, Gene, was in the Air Force and was stationed there and they went to visit Gene. They stopped in England, for some sight seeing. That was when David's suitcase was lost and he had to ware just two sets of clothes the rest of trip. He wore one set while the other was in the laundry.
This is one the most memorial parts of the trip for him.

David graduated from Alleghany County High School at the age of sixteen. He was active in the drama club all through high school and was in many plays.

David entered Catawba college in Salisbury, North Carolina at the age of sixteen and graduated with a Bachelor of Arts degree in the performing arts May 1986, he was twenty years old. While attending college he received many awards for achievement in drama.

He has worked in theater related jobs since his graduation, mostly in lighting design. His work has allowed him to travel to South America and visit several countries there. At this time David is working for the Virginia Opera Company, in Norfolk, Virginia as a lighting designer.

David and Karen Oberthal, have plans to marry 22 April 1995, at Sacred Heart Church, Norfolk. Virginia. For the present time they will make their home in Norfolk, Virginia.

SANDY O'NEAL[10] **HAMMACK**, (Betty Sue[10] **STAMPER**), (Onley[9]), (John (Ander) Andrew[8]), (Troy[7]), (Hiram H.[6]), (John[5]), (Jonathan Jr.[4]), (Jonathan Sr.[3]), (Powell[2]), (John[1]) came to live with Betty Sue Stamper Latham and George Henry Latham, as a foster child on 25 August 1976. He was born on 29 May 1966 in Danbury, North Carolina. Sandy was born premature and weighted only two and a half pounds, his mother left him in the hospital. He knows that his mother's maiden name was Lawson, he knows nothing about his father. He has been told that his father was not the Hammack man his mother was married to. Sandy lived with Betty and George until he was over eighteen years old. Though he was not adopted or did not change his name to Latham he was always thought of as a son by all the family.

Sandy moved to Florida to work when he was eighteen years old and lived there for several years. He learned a trade in machinery while working in Florida.

Sandy married Susan Elizabeth Hilbert on 8 September 1988. in Englewood, Florida. Susan was born in Florida, her parents were Harvey Hilbert and Jean (do not have maiden name) Hilbert. When Sandy married he asked his father George Henry Latham to be his best man. George felt that this was an honor. Sandy's mother Betty made his wedding cake.

Sandy did find his older brother Jerry Hammack. Jerry and his family moved in a house beside Sandy and Susan. Sandy and Jerry had very little in common and after about a year Jerry and family moved to another state. Sandy now knows that his birth mother lives in Florida, but he has never meet her.

Sandy and Susan moved from Florida to Alleghany County, North Carolina. This year Sandy and Susan had a house built at Mountain View. They live near George and Betty Latham and frequently have Sunday dinner with them. Sandy now has his own company running a ditching service.

JOHN DANIEL[11] **HARRIS**, (Shirley Jean[10] **STAMPER**), (Onley[9]), (John (Ander) Andrew[8]), (Troy[7]), (Hiram H.[6]), (John[5]), (Jonathan Jr.[4]), (Jonathan Sr.[3]), (Powell[2]), (John[1]) is the oldest son of Shirley Jean Stamper Harris and Olen Vaughn Harris. John was born on 28 April 1958 in Sparta, North Carolina.

As a boy John loved horses and rode and showed them. The family owned Tennessee Walking horses. John worked as a butcher for a local grocery while going to high school. He is a graduate of Alleghany County High School.

While in high school John was very active in drama. He acted in many plays as well as directed them. He graduated from Catawaba College in Salisbury, North Carolina, with a degree in the Performing Arts. The year after he graduated he acted and worked on the set for "Horn In The West", a summer outdoor drama, in Boone, North Carolina. After that he moved to San Antonio, Texas and worked in dinner theaters, he moved to Houston, Texas and worked in theaters there. Since that his work has been in the theater or opera.

John Daniel Harris married Betty (Jane) Senter on 28 May 1976, at Chestnut Grove Church, in Alleghany county, North Carolina. They had one stillbirth child on 29 August 1977, a girl they named Regina. The baby was buried at Mount Caramel church cemetery. John and Jane got a divorce soon after this.

John married Teresa Minton from Wilkes County, North Carolina on 31 December 1981. Teresa is the daughter of Millard Minton and Shelvie Jean Swain Minton . John and Teresa have two children:
(1) Jeana Daniel born on 12 April 1987 in San Antonio, Texas.
(2) Zachary Thomas born on 9 April 1992, in Wilkesboro, North Carolina.

John now works for the Virginia Opera Company as a set designer and stage manager in Norfolk, Virginia. Teresa works as a home interior decorator and in real estate.

MARK VAUGHN[11] HARRIS, (Shirley Jean[10] **STAMPER**), (Onley[9]), (John (Ander) Andrew[8]), (Troy[7]), (Hiram H.[6]), (John[5]), (Jonathan Jr.[4]), (Jonathan Sr.[3]), (Powell[2]), (John[1]) is the youngest son of Shirley Jean Stamper Harris and Olen Vaughn Harris. Mark was born on 15 February 1962, in Sparta, North Carolina.

Mark is a graduate of Alleghany County High School. While in high school he was active in sports, he was on the football team and wrestling team. He graduated from Appalachian College in Boone, North Carolina. He works in sales for a trucking company.

Mark married Kimberly (Kim) Michelle Gregory on 1 December 1990, in Mocksville, North Carolina. Mark's father Olen Harris was his best man. Kim's father is James W. Gregory Jr. do not have her mother's name. Kim works for the U S Air. Mark and Kim live in Kernersville, North Carolina. Mark and Kim's first child, Gregory (Luke) Harris, was born 4 January 1995.

PAMELA S.[11] STAMPER, (John Edward[10]), (Linville[9]), (John (Ander) Andrew[6]), (Troy[7]), (Hiram H.[6]), (John[5]), (Jonathan Jr.[4]), (Jonathan Sr.[3]), (Powell[2]), (John[1]) is the oldest child of John Edward Stamper and Cora Mae Ramey Stamper. She was born 13 August 1954 in Surry county, North Carolina. Pamela married Lars Erik Brandt on 23 October 1982. Lares Erik was born 26 April 1952 in Stockholm, Sweden. His parents are Erik Hjalmar Brandt and Ulla Maria Petterson Brandt they were both born in Sweden and Ulla still live there. Erik Hjalmar died a few years ago.

The Brandt family have a family tradition of naming the male children with Erik as part of their name. It could be some kind of Swedish tradition. Lares Erik is a pilot for the American Airlines.

Pamela S. Stamper Brandt and Lares Erik Brandt have two sons: (1) Erik (Cory) born on 24 July 1983. Erik Cory is called Cory. Cory loves to play hockey and is very good at it, for his age, he has played in several torments. (2) Edward (Erik) born on 26 January 1992, is called Erik, he a beautiful blond who looks Swedish.

Pamela is interested in family research and has been to Middlesex County and to Stamper's Landing, Virginia. She went with Betty Stamper Latham to Ash County Courthouse, in Jefferson, North Carolina, to look through old deed and will books.

MICHAEL[11] **STAMPER**, (Lonzo[10]), (Schley (Bert)[9]), (John (Ander) Andrew[8]), (Troy[7]), (Hiram H.[6]), (John[5]), (Jonathan Jr.[4]), (Jonathan Sr.[3]), (Powell[2]), (John[1]) is the oldest son of Lonzo and Elsie Gentry Stamper. He was born on 26 July 1951 in Hartford county, Beg Air, Maryland. Michael married Linda Whitehead on 1 September 1978. They have two children; (1) Caudae, she was born on 16 april 1986. (2) Chad, he was born on 27 July 1987. Chad is a young male Stamper who will cary on the Stamper name.

DAVID[11] **STAMPER**, (Lonzo[10]), (Schley (Bert)[9]), (John (Ander)Andrew[8]), (Troy[7]), (Hiram H.[6]), (John[5]), (Jonathan Jr.[4]), (Jonathan Sr.[3]), (Powell[2]), (John[1]) is the son of Lonzo and Elsie Gentry Stamper. He was born on 18 January 1953 in Belair, Maryland. He married Debbie Plummer on 24 May 1977 and later they divorced.

LARRY[11] **STAMPER**, (Lonzo[10]), (Schley (Bert)[9]), (John (Ander) Andrew[8]), (Troy[7]), (John[5]), (Jonathan Jr.[4]), (Jonathan Sr.[3]), (Powell[2]), (John [1]) is the son of Lonzo and Elsie Gentry Stamper. He was born on 27 March 1959 in Beg Air, Maryland. He married Julia Bennett on 26 January 1980. Larry and Julia had three children before they divorced. Their children are; (1) Sarah, she was born on 10 October 1980, (2) Ryan, he was born on 24 April 1985, and (3) Jesse, he was born on 9 April 1986. Ryan and Jesse are young male Stampers to cary on the Stamper name.

CAROLYN ANN[11] **GREENBURG**, (Elaine[10] **STAMPER**), (Schley (Bert)[9]), (John (Ander) Andrew[8]), (Troy[7]), (Hiram H.[6]), (John[5]), (Jonathan Jr.[4]), Jonathan Sr, [3]), (Powell[2]), (John[1]) is the daughter of Elaine Stamper Greenburg and Charles William Greenburg. She was born on 16 November 1947, in Maryland. She married Raphael Vendett and had two children, they later divorced.

Carolyn and Raphael Vendett's children are; (1) Anthony Douglas born on 11 July 1971, (2) Carli Angela born on 28 June 1974.

Carolyn married Kenneth J. Walls on 28 September 1991. They live in Maryland near Carolyn's mother Elaine Stamper Greenburg.

CHARLES WILLIAM[11] GREENBURG JR., (Elaine[10] **STAMPER**), (Schley (Bert)[9]), (John (Ander) Andrew[8]), (Troy[7]), (Hiram H.[6]), (John[5]), (Jonathan Jr.[4]), (Jonathan Sr.[3]), (Powell[2]), (John[1]), is the son of Elaine Stamper Greenburg and Charles William Greenburg Sr. He was born on 30 August 1952. On 14 October 1972 Charles married Deborah Jean Schiller and they had three children. Charles and Deborah's children are: (1) Jana Nicole born on 20 June 1977 in Richmond, Virginia, (2) Andrea Morgan born on 18 June 1980 in Richmond, Virginia, and (3) Katherine Elaine born on March 1989 in Richmond, Virginia. The family lives in Richmond, Virginia.

BRIAN PHILIP[11] GREENBURG, (Elaine[10] **STAMPER**), (Schley (Bert)[9]), (John (Ander) Andrew[8]), (Troy[7]), (Hiram H.[6]), (John[5]), (Jonathan Jr.[4]), (Jonathan Sr, [3]), (Powell[2]), (John[1]) is the son of Elaine Stamper Greenburg and Charles William Greenburg Sr. He was born on 10 August 1955 in Maryland. Brian married Susan Roberta Hoxter and they had two children. (1) Brannan Matthew born on 11 January 1980 in Houston, Texas. (2) Shannan Leigh born on 23 April 1982 in Houston, Texas. The family lives in Houston, Texas.

DEBBIE MAE[11] STARR, (Norma[10] **STAMPER**), (Schley (Bert)[9]), (John (Ander) Andrew[8]), (Troy[7]), (Hiram H.[6]), (John[5]), (Jonathan Jr.[4]), (Jonathan Sr.[3]) (Powell[2]), (John[1]), is the daughter of Norma Stamper Starr and Marshall (Sonny) Starr. She was born on 29 November 1954 in Maryland. Debbie married Jami Melani on 11 February 1978. Debbie and Jami had three sons; (1) Jason Kirk born on 18 April 1979, (2) Jeremy Carl born on 20 Jan 1981, and (3) Joshua Brant born on 11 March 1982. The family lives in Maryland near Norma and Sonny.

MARSHA (KAREN)[11] STARR, (Norma[10] **STAMPER**), (Schely (Bert)[9]), (John (Ander) Andrew[8]), (Troy[7]), (Hiram H.[6]), (John[5]), (Jonathan Jr.[4]), (Jonathan Sr.[3]), (Powell[2]), (John[1]) is the daughter of Norma Stamper Starr and Marshall (Sonny) Starr. She was born on 21 June 1956 in Maryland. On 14 October 1977 she married Paul Thomas Walker. They have three sons; (1) Zachery Charles born on 28 January 1980, (2) Travis Evan born on 14 August 1985, and (3) Seth Thomas born on 13 April 1987. The family lives in Maryland near Norma and Sonny.

CONNIE ANN[11] STARR, (Norma[10] **STAMPER**), (Schely (Bert)[9]), (John (Ander) Andrew[8]), (Troy[7]), (Hiram H.[6]), (John[5]), (Jonathan Jr.[4]), (Jonathan Sr, [3]), (Powell[2]), (John[1]) is the daughter if Norma Stamper Starr and Marshal (Sonny) Starr and was born on 20 August 1958. Connie married James Joseph Turek on 30 June 1984. James was born on 23 March 1947. Connie and James have one child James Marshall born on 23 July 1991 in Maryland.

JOHN (RANDY)[11] MILES, (Wade Van[10] Miles), (Virdie Alice[9] **STAMPER**), (John (Ander) Andrew[8]), (Troy[7]), (Hiram[6]), (John[5]), (Jonathan Jr.[4]), (Jonathan Sr.[3]), (Powell[2]), (John[1]), the son of Wade Van Miles and Jamalee (Jo) Franklin Miles was born on 2 July 1947. He married Wanda Brooks and they have two children.

Randy and Wanda's children are: (1) Charles Austin born on 10 October 1970 and (2) Cassandra Lynn born on 24 February 1976. Randy retired from Lowes Building Supply Company in 1993. He now works in South Carolina.

ANGELA[11] MILES, (Wade Van[10] Miles), (Virdie Alice[9] **STAMPER**), (John (Ander) Andrew[8]), (Troy[7]), (Hiram[6]), (John[5]), (Jonathan Jr.[4]), (Jonathan Sr.[3]), (Powell[2]), (John[1]) is the daughter of Wade Vane Miles and Jamalee (Jo) Franklin Miles, she was born on 8 December 1950 in Alleghany County, North Carolina. Angela married James R. Gentry, they have two children. Their children are: (1) James Richard Gentry born about 1970, he married Crystal Armstrong. James and Crystal have a son, James Dakota, born 1994. (2) Sebrina Jo Gentry we do not have her birth date. Angela and James live just across the road from Angela's mother.

ANETTA LYNN[11] MILES, (John Thomas (Tom)[10] Miles), (Virdie Alice[9] **STAMPER**), (John Andrew (Ander)[8]), (Troy[7]), (Hiram H.[6]), (John[5]), (Jonathan Jr.[4]), (Jonathan Sr.[3]), (Powell[2]), (John[1]) is the daughter of John Thomas (Tom) and Shirley Lee Wagnor Miles. She was born on 21 February 1955. She is a Pharmacy Technician at a pharmacy in Statesville, North Carolina. She married Eric Thorton Dailey. Eric is an Executive at Intercraft Industries in Statesville, North Carolina. Anetta and Eric had two children; (1) Jennifer Lee Dailey, at this time on 3 September 1994 she is a Junior at Salem College. She is the reigning Miss Iredell County, North Carolina. (2) David Joshua (Josh) Dailey at this time is a sophomore in high school and plays football for the Jayvee Team. They are a Christian family.

JODY THEODORE[11] MILES, (John Thomas (Tom)[10] Miles), (Verdie Alice[9] **STAMPER**), (John Andrew (Ander)[8]), (Troy[7]), (Hiram H.[6]), (John[5]), (Jonathan Jr.[4]), (Jonathan Sr.[3]), (Powell[2]), (John[1]) is the son of John Thomas (Tom) and Shirley Lee Wagoner. He was born on 10 January 1967.

Jody served six years in the National Guard and specialized in the infantry. He married Angela Christine Sloan. They had three children; (1) Leah born 1989, (2) Jacob born 1991 and (3) John Walter Miles IV born 1993. The family lives in Statesville, North Carolina.

STANLEY PHILLIP (PHIL)[11] EDWARDS, (Mary Lou[10] Miles), (Virdie Alice[9]**STAMPER**), (John (Ander) Andrew[8]), (Troy[7]), (Hiram[6]), (John[5]), (Jonathan Jr.[4]), (Jonathan Sr.[3]), (Powell[2]), (John[1]) was the third child of Mary Lou Miles and Westly (Herbert) Edwards. He was born on 12 February 1951. He married Beverly Caudle on 5 August 1972. Phil and Beverly had two children (1) Kristy Camelle born 17 November 1972. Kristy married Darel Byrd on 27 April 1994. (2) Westly Miles was born on 22 April 1976. Phil is the pastor of New Covenant Church in Ennice,North Carolina.

VERNON MARTIN (MARTY)[11] **ROYAL**), (Nancy[10] Miles), (Virdie Alice[9] **STAMPER**), (John (Ander) Andrew[8]), (Troy[7]), (Hiram[6]), (John[5]), (Jonathan Jr.[4]), (Jonathan Sr.[3]), (Powell[2]), (John[1]) is the son of Nancy Miles Royal he was born 20 March 1962. He married Patsy Andrews from Mt. Airy, North Carolina. That is where they live, at this time. Marty and Patsy have two children: (1) Nathan and (2) Michael Paul.

Often on weekends Marty goes to Sparta and takes his mother, Nancy, home with him to spend the weekend. He and Patsy take her shopping. Nancy does not get out much because of her severe arthritis.

SHERRY LYDIA[11] **ROYAL**, (Nancy[10] Miles), (Verdie Alice[9] **STAMPER**), (John (Ander) Andrew[8]), (Troy[7]), (Hiram[6]), (John[5]), (Jonathan Jr.[4]), (Jonathan Sr.[3]), (Powell[2]), (John[1]) is the daughter of Nancy Miles Royal and Willie G. Royal. She was born on 29 September 1966. She married Jerry Chastain and had two children. Her children are (1) William (Andrew) and (2) Shanna. Sherry and Jerry divorced. William (Andrew) lives with Sherry and Shanna lives with Jerry and his parents. Sherry is now living with her mother, Nancy, as she is needed there to help care for Nancy.

MARGARET ANN[11] **EVANS**, (Margaret (Louise)[10] Miles), (Minnie Inez (Ine)[9] **STAMPER**), (John (Ander) Andrew[8]), (Troy[7]), (Hiram H.[6]), (John[5]), (Jonathan Jr.[4]), (Jonathan Sr.[3]), (Powell[2]), (John[1]) is the oldest child of Margaret (Louise) Miles Evans and Samuel Clifton (Cliff) Evans. She was born on 24 April 1942 in Alleghany County, North Carolina.

She graduated from Alleghany county High School and went to college. She was the private secretary to the Administrator of Alleghany County Memorial Hospital. After his retirement she became the Administrator and held that position for several years. Later she gave up that position and became the owner and manager of the Pizzeria Restaurant in Sparta, North Carolina.

Margaret married James Willard Cox on 11 February 1961. James was born on 5 December 1938. Margaret and James had three children. (1) James Christopher (Chris) born on 30 November 1961. Chris married Carole Elizabeth Finger on 12 August 1989. (2) Lisa Ann was born on 25 March 1964. Lisa Ann married three times; Billy Maines, Mark Douglas Wyatt and on 30 August 1992 she married Tommy Billings. Lias Ann has two children at this time they are Kathelyn Louise Wyatt and James Adam Maines. (3) Jeffery Alen was born on 31 October 1968.

Margaret and James divorced. After the divorce, Margaret married Carroll Crouse and they own and manage the Pizzeria Restaurant in Sparta, North Carolina.

SANDRA LEE[11] EVANS, (Margaret (Louise)[10] Miles),(Minnie (Inez)[9] **STAMPER,** (John (Ander) Andrew[8]), (Troy[7]), (Hiram H.[6]), (John[5]), (Jonathan Jr.[4]), (Jonathan[3]), (Powell[2]), (John[1]), is the second child of Margaret (Louise) Miles Evans and Samuel (Clifton (Cliff) Evans, she was born on 19 December 1945. Sandra first married Jerry Taylor about 1965, they divorced. Sandra married Harold Carter on 14 June 1974. Harold was born on 26 May 1932[7]. Sandra's children are; (1) Linda Lee, do not have birth date. She married Rick Erclandson. Her son is Garrett Lee Erclandson. (2) Catherine Inez, do not have birth date. She married Jim Hunter. Her children are (a) Ashley and (b) Dylon. (3) Raivena Louis, do not have birth date. She married Scott Hughes. Her children are; (a) Stephanie, (b) Jessica, (c) Carter and (d) Scott. (4) Christine Louise, do not have her birth date. She married Michael Calhoun. Her children are (a) Louise and (b) Benjamin.

SAMUEL (SAM) CLIFTON[11] EVANS JR, (Margaret (Louise)[10] Miles), (Minnie (Inez)[9] **STAMPER**), (John (Ander) Andrew[8]), (Troy[7]), (Hiram H.[6]) (John[5]), (Jonathan Jr.[4]), (Jonathan Sr.[3]), (Powell[2]), (John[1]), the only son of Louise Miles Evans and Samuel Clifton (Cliff) Evans Sr. was born on 21 November 1949. Samuel (Sam) Clifton Evans Jr. married Sun Lee Doughton and they had two sons; (1) Jason Doughton Evans born on 20 August 1976, and (2) Patrick Clayton Evans born on 14 January 1984. Sam died on 26 May 1986 from an accident while riding a bicycle along the Blue Ridge Parkway. He was a brilliant young Lawyer with a bright future.

HAROLD DEAN[11] MILES, (John (Junior) Raymond[10] Miles Jr.), (Minnie(Inez)[9] **STAMPER**), (John (Ander) Andrew[8]), (Troy[7]), (Hiram H.[6]), (John[5]), (Jonathan Jr.[4]), (Jonathan Sr.[3]) (Powell[1]), (John[1]), the son of John (Junior) Raymond Miles and Earlene Joines Miles was born on 23 August 1944. He married Linda Ann Nichalson on 28 January 1968. Linda Ann was born on 8 July 1947. Their children are (1) Dianna Lynn born on 4 June 1970, and (2) Julie Marie born on January 1978.

LARRY DAVID[11] MILES, (John (Junior) Raymond[10] Miles Jr.), (Minnie (Inez)[9] **STAMPER,** (John (Ander) Andrew[8]), (Troy[7]), (Hiram H.[6]), (John[5]), (Jonathan Jr.[4]), (Jonathan Sr, [3]), (Powell[2]), John[1]) the son of John (Junior) Raymond Miles and Earlene Joines Miles was born on 23 July 1946. He married Vickie Lynn Saunders on 5 June 1971. Vickie Lynn was born on 27 November 1952. Their children are (1) Matthew born on 30 April 1973, and (2) Jennifer Lynn born 19 April 1978.

WANDA LYNN[11] MILES, (John (Junior) Raymond[10] Miles Jr.), (Minnie (Inez)[9] **STAMPER**), (John (Ander) Andrew[8]), (Troy[7]), (Hiram H.[6]), (John[5]), (Jonathan Jr.[4]), (Jonathan Sr.[3]), (Powell[2]), (John[1]) the daughter of John (Junior) Raymond Miles and Earlene Joines Miles was born on 16 June 1956. She married John (Ray) Rayvon Shaw on 27 July 1974. Ray was born on 1 February 1953, he is the son of James Shaw and Olen Todd Shaw. He is a very good musician and has had several LP albums and tapes recorded. Wanda and Ray's children are (1) Meghann Leah born on 31 July 1977, and (2) David Jarrod born on 26 March 1981.

JOHN (MARTY) MARTIN[11] MILES, (John (Junior) Raymond[10] Miles), (Minnie (Inez)[9] **STAMPER**), (John (Ander) Andrew[8]), (Troy[7]), (Hiram H.[6]), John[5]), (Jonathan Jr.[4]), (Jonathan Sr.[3]), (Powell[2]), (John[1]) the son of John (Junior) Raymond Miles and Earlene Joines Miles was born on 18 November 1963. He married Charlotte Ann Edwards on 29 August 1987. Marty and Charlotte's children are (1) John Ethan born on 14 January 1990, and (2) Carl Adrian born on 28 August 1991.

RODNEY GENE[11] STAMPER, (Warren Lincoln[10]), (William Harrison[9]), (Abraham[8]), (Masterson (Bad Mat[7]), (Jean (Jennie)[6]Stamper), (Joshua Sr.[5]), (Jonathan Jr.[4]), (Jonathan Sr.[3]), (Powell[2]), (John[1]) is the son of Warren Lincoln Stamper and Helen (Thelma) Adams Stamper. He was born on 7 December 1959 in Arlington, Virginia. He moved with his parents to Sparta, North Carolina when he was a teenager. Rodney married Nancy Ellen Millinax and they live in Atlanta, Georgia. Rodney and Nancy have a son Gregory Michael, he was born on 2 October 1989.

GREGORY[12] STAMPER, the son of Rodney Gene Stamper, who is now five years old visits his grandmother Thelma Stamper, in Sparta, North Carolina. Gregory's grandfather, Warren Stamper died before he was born. Gregory lives in Atlanta, Georgia with his parents. He is excited about visiting his grandmother, at Easter time. Grandma will help him hunt Easter eggs and she will play catch with him. Grandma will play any game he wants to play. Gregory and his grandmother play catch in the back yard, on a warm, sunny, April day. Grandma troughs the ball to Gregory and he misses it and the dog chases the ball. Gregory starts to chase the dog but instead he runs and hugs his grandmother. Gregory and Grandma laugh as they hug each other, it is a good day to be alive. It is a good day to be a five year old Stamper boy.

Other **STAMPERS:**

There were Stampers living in Philadelphia, Pennsylvania, before 1750. John and Hannah Stamper lived in Philadelphia in 1726. John was a successful merchant and he became Mayor in 1759. He had a brother named Joseph. It is believed that these Stampers came from Germany[13].

There were some Stampers in Wilkes County that have not been placed as of yet. We have a James Stamper born about 1777, Margaret, Mary and Rachel born between 1798 and 1805.

FINIS M. STAMPER born about 1900, a Randolph County, Kentucky school teacher, turned to part time egg and poultry selling to support his growing family. In the early years he shipped live chickens to markets in St. Louis and Kansas City. During World War II his company sold canned chickens to the military. Later the canned chicken became the first supermarket product with the Banquet label. By the early 1950's an experimental product, Banquet frozen chicken pies, were started and led the way to radical changes in the company. Today we see many kinds of cooked frozen chickens and frozen dinners with the Banquet label.

ROD STAMPER: In Rapid City, South Dakota, Stampers own the Stamper Black Hills Gold Jewelry Company. The story of the Stampers is a story of western pioneer spirit with strong ties to excellence and tradition. For several generations the Stamper family has been making tri-color jewelry, following a tradition which goes back many centuries. Rod Stamper personally cuts and inspects all the molds used to stamp the leaves and grapes, used in the making of tri-colored jewelry. The factory and offices are located in the foothills along the main highway to Mount Rushmore.

"....and departing leave behind us, footprints in the sands of time"

- Henry Wadsworth Longfellow
"Psalm of Life"

STAMPER FOOTPRINTS A STORY WITHOUT END

SOURCES AND NOTES

[1] "Parish Register of Christ Church, Middlesex County, Virginia 1653 - 1812". Published by the National Society of the Colonial Dames of America in the State of Virginia. Richmond: William Ellis Jones, Steam Book and Job Printer 1897. Last reprint for Clearfield Company Inc. by Genealogical Publishing Co Inc. Baltimore, Maryland 1990.

[2] Stamper, Dr. Clifford. Morganton, North Carolina.
Personal research and Family tradition.

[3] Rutman, Darrett B. and Anita H. Rutman. "A Place in Time Middlesex County, Virginia 1650 - 1750". New York; Norton, 1984.

[4] "Vestry Book Of Christ Church Parish, Middlesex County, Virginia, 1663 - 1767".
There are two copies of this book in the library in Urbanna, Virginia.

[5] Sebastian, Samuel E. Wilkesboro, North Carolina.
Personal research.

[6] Moore, Corneal Lynn B., Fairfax, Virginia.
Personal research.

[7] "Alleghany County Heritage - North Carolina".
Alleghany Historical - Genealogical Society, Inc. Sparta, North Carolina. Printed by Hunter Publishing Company, Winston-Salem, North Carolina, 1983.

[8] Latham, George H, Glade Valley, North Carolina
Personal research.

[9] Alderman, John Perry, "Carroll/Grayson Marriages 1793 - 1852".
Alderman Books, Hillsville, Virginia.

[10] "Ashe County Heritage - North Carolina".
Ashe Historical - Genealogical Society, Inc. West Jefferson, North Carolina. Printed by Hunter Publishing Company, Winston-Salem, North Carolina.

[11] Harris, Shirley Stamper. "Roses Beyond The Sunset".
Sparta, North Carolina, 1989.

[12] Grogan, Hiram, Symrna, Georgia.
Personal research and Family Tradition

[13] Meadows, Helen, Shade Springs, West Virginia.
Family Tradition.

[14] The Church of the Latter Day Saints, Library
Rockville, Maryland.

[15] Gray, Louise, Evelyn O. Ryland, and Bettie J. Simmons. "Historic Buildings in Middlesex County, Virginia, 1650 - 1875", Chelorre, North Carolina; Delmar Printing Company.

[16] Maynard, Betty M., "Stamper Court Records Middlesex County, Virginia, 1673 - 1852". Danville, Virginia, 1989.

[17] Stamper, James J., Independence, Virginia. Personal research.

[18] Cox, A. B., "Footprints on the Sands of Time: A history of Southwestern, Virginia and Northwestern, North Carolina". Sparta, North Carolina: Star Publishing Company, 1900.

NAME INDEX

All names cited in the text are listed in the index. Married women are listed under the maiden name and all married names. Names appear in capitals or lower case depending on their appearance in the text. This difference is without significance. The numbers in this index refer to page numbers.

www.ingramcontent.com/pod-product-compliance
Lightning Source LLC
Chambersburg PA
CBHW080615270326
41928CB00016B/3067
9780788403200